热爱

Soul Development **Soul Study**

Soul Communication

Soul Healing

A Guide to
Soul Journey Accessing your
Highest Powers

Soul Enlightment

may 8, 2003

Soul Study

A Guide to Accessing your Highest Powers

Zhi Gang Sha
(Xiao Gang Guo)

ZHI NENG PRESS
VANCOUVER, BC

Any application of the material in this book is at the
reader's discretion and sole responsibility. Distress of
any kind during or after performing any of the exercises
in this book should be carefully monitored as it may indicate
a problem that requires the attention of a health-care professional.

Soul Study
A Guide to Accessing Your Highest Powers

For further information:

Zhi Neng Press

International Institute of Zhi Neng™ Medicine
   Box #60583
   Granville Park PO
   Vancouver, BC, Canada
   V6H 4B9

   In North America, call toll-free: 1-888-339-6815.

Published by Zhi Neng Press

First published   July 1996
   2nd Printing   January 1997
   3rd Printing   April 1998

ISBN 0-9680595-1-1

cover design: Heaven

direction: Master Zhi Gang Sha

cover illustration: Anand R. Mani

book design, layout and visuals: Jim YC Chow

printing: Benwell-Atkins

i

Master Zhi Chen Guo, founder of Zhi Neng medicine.
photo courtesy of Master Sha

Master Zhi Gang Sha, founder of *Sha's Acupuncture Therapy*.
photo courtesy of Master Sha

**Master Zhi Chen Guo (right) and Master Zhi Gang Sha.
Shijiazhuang, Tian Jing, China, October, 1994.**
photo courtesy of Master Sha

Master Sha with his new family on the day of his adoption. October, 1993.
photo courtesy of Master Sha

Master Guo (2nd from left), Master Sha, Sylvia Chen, Mei Ling Guo, Miriam Leung Rotenburg.
photo courtesy of Master Sha

Dedication

This book is dedicated to people who seek to know their soul and access their highest powers. Through soul study, soul communication and soul healing, may they find fulfillment and enlightenment.

Acknowledgments

First of all, I would like to thank my master and adoptive father, Zhi Chen Guo; my adoptive mother, Jin Ying Jiang Guo; my adoptive grandmother and five sisters; and the many saints in the soul world for supporting and nourishing me, my disciples and the students who participated in the first Soul Study course. This program started on March 1st, 1996 in Vancouver, and was the first to be held in the Western world.

Special appreciation goes to Sylvia Chen and her family for supporting my work for the past four years. Sylvia's contribution, commitment and full support are deeply appreciated.

In the production of this book, I am very appreciative of my disciples and students. I am deeply grateful to May Guey Chew for writing and compiling the book from my dictation and the taped classroom proceedings of the first Soul Study program. I thank the editing team of Diana Holland, Diana Bennest, Steven James Wong, May Guey Chew and Jim Chow for bringing the book to this polished state. I thank Jim Chow for the design and layout of this book. The five of them united as one team, giving from their hearts and losing much sleep. No words can express the appreciation I have for their contribution. Thank you.

I appreciate other disciples and students for supporting the production of the book in their own way, including Sharon Soubolsky, Benedito José Da Silva, Brigida Milne, Bozena Sacha, Diane Clair Lafrenière, Tammy Tran, Yuan Yuan, Nathalie Thomann and Troy Davids.

For rescuing the computers and doing whatever he could to support my work, I thank Colin Williams.

I thank my wife, Qion Xi Luo Sha, my children, my parents and my in-laws for their continued support.

In closing, I sincerely thank all my disciples, students, friends, and patients for supporting my work in Zhi Neng medicine and Soul Study. Thank you very much.

Thank you.

Zhi Gang Sha
Vancouver, BC
June 26, 1996

Contents

Chapter One. Soul Basics

Chapter Two. Techniques for Soul Development and Communication

Chapter Three. Applying the Power of the Soul in Your Life

Conclusion

Testimonials and Comments

Appendices

Figures and Tables

Introduction

This book opens the knowledge of soul study, the highest science in the universe, to the public. Many people talk about soul development, soul communication and soul healing. There are many books available on the subject. Every Master, writer, and spiritual leader has a different idea. There is much we do not know, much we cannot understand.

Therefore, we study, we learn, we experience what the soul world is: we do soul study.

In Taoist philosophy, *"The Tao produces One, One produces Two, Two produces Three, and Three produces all things."* As such, this book has been arranged into three chapters. Chapter One, *Soul Basics,* gives you principles and knowledge of the soul and the soul world. Chapter Two, *Techniques For Soul Development and Communication,* gives you the techniques you need to develop your soul and communicate with the soul world and the universe. Chapter Three, *Applying the Power of the Soul in Your Life,* describes some of the benefits soul knowledge will bring to your health, business and general well-being.

This book introduces some of the deepest secrets of the universe. I have written it in plain language as it is meant to be a learning aid. It gives you basic knowledge of the soul and the soul world, and provides the tools you need to lay the groundwork for your future enlightenment.

Take this key and unlock the door to the universe.

Before You Start...

The training presented in this book was first developed in China by Master Zhi Chen Guo, the founder of Zhi Neng medicine. I, Zhi Gang Sha, am the first disciple and adopted son of Master Guo, his representative in the Western world, and the only Master to teach Soul Study outside of China.

My responsibility as a Master is to ensure that my students and disciples embark upon their journey of enlightenment safely and with proper guidance.

In a classroom setting, I would talk with each of your souls to ensure that your soul study will be very successful. To you, my reader, I wish the same success.

The first principle to follow is not to expect anything. You must allow time for things to flow and develop naturally. You must take time to learn your *ABC's* before you can go on to higher levels of soul development. What I teach in this book and in my Soul Study classes is a revolutionary way to develop soul communication and soul healing.

Let us begin...

Chapter One

Soul Basics

I. The Soul

The soul is the essence of life.

I. The Mind, Body and Soul Relationship

Everything in the universe has a soul, both living things and inanimate things. Human beings consist of two parts – the physical body and the soul.

The soul resides inside the human body. It is the essence of life. The soul has all the functions and traits that a human being has, and more. The soul has its own thoughts and emotions, its own personality, form, shape and weight. You can see your own soul and that of others if you have developed your Third Eye[1] function.

---

[1] Called the Third Eye by Buddhists and the Upper Dan Tian by Taoists, this energy area in the body needs to be developed to enhance the capabilities of the mind. Anatomically, the pineal gland coincides with the location of the Third Eye.

The soul is an independent system that thinks and functions inside the body. The physical body consists of organs such as the heart, lungs, kidneys and brain. The control centre for the physical body is the brain, which includes the conscious and subconscious minds. It controls all the organs in the body. The brain is part of the physical body, but the soul is independent of it. The soul, the conscious mind, and the subconscious mind are three separate but related entities.

Generally speaking, the mind is defined as roughly 80% brain functioning and 20% soul functioning. The conscious mind and the subconscious mind represent the surface and deeper levels of brain function respectively. The soul directs the subconscious mind, which directs the conscious mind, which then orders the physical body to take action.

Souls have personalities. They are intelligent, sensitive, and emotional, and they have minds of their own. They have their own likes and dislikes, desires and biases, personalities and quirks. When their souls are happy, people are also happy, calm, peaceful, and serene in their lives. When their souls are unhappy, people are often upset, depressed and miserable. Many emotional problems are directly related to conflicts between the mind and the soul.

For example, the soul may direct a person to take up soul study. The subconscious mind agrees, saying, *"Yes, that is a good idea. I want to learn also."* The subconscious mind sends a message to the conscious mind. The conscious mind agrees and the person acts on the message.

Alternately, in answer to the subconscious mind's directive to take up soul study, the conscious mind may reply, *"I cannot afford to do that right now."* In this case, the conscious mind blocks the soul's wish. Neither the conscious mind nor the subconscious mind necessarily follow the soul's directives.

5

If there is long-term conflict or disagreement between mind and soul, the soul will suffer hurt and dissatisfaction. Its growth can be stunted. If his or her soul gets upset or very sad, a person may experience depression, sickness, sadness. People may function less well in their lives and realize less of their potential when the soul is not being allowed to develop. In extreme cases, when the soul's desires are thwarted constantly by the subconscious or the conscious mind, mental disorder can result. In most cases of depression, the root cause is conflict with the soul.

Some people have a miserable childhood. Their parents may beat them, shout and yell at them all the time. They may suffer from physical abuse, sexual abuse or inadequate love, which impoverishes and weakens their soul. Often, their souls get scared, frightened, upset and traumatized. They get sick. Some souls sicken to the point where they do not want to stay in this world anymore. Suicidal tendencies surface. The sick soul may say, *"Jump off the bridge."* The conscious mind may say, *"No. My life is not finished yet,"* and this conversation may go on many times. One day, the message to go is too strong and life ends.

2. The Soul Seeks New Knowledge

The soul needs to develop and gain experience in every life. Normally, it is inside your body, absorbing energy and information from the universe. The soul seldom leaves the body, but it does go where it will to fulfill its needs and its higher purpose. This may occur for only a few minutes at a time, once or twice a day, but the soul hungers for new knowledge so much that you cannot stop it from seeking what it needs to find. It leaves and then returns once it has finished attending to its needs. Without the soul, the body is unmoving, just like wood. When the soul returns, you can move again.

The soul goes anywhere it needs to go. For example, there are more than 10,000 souls listening in during my Soul Study class. Many souls have flown here to learn what I teach. Some have come because their saint guide told them to come. Others are here because their needs have brought them. Soul study is good for the soul.

Different lives are like different classes. There are many lessons to be learned and many levels of learning to go through. The soul gets happier and happier as it progresses through each stage of development.

3. What Is Soul Language?

Soul language is a language unique to your soul that is brought out with special training. Every soul speaks in a different way and brings out language in a voice that people do not understand unless they have been trained to translate. Soul language is not senseless babble, nor can you produce it at will by using your conscious mind.

Soul language is a voice that you develop when you repeat, very fast, the Zhi Neng medicine universal healing number, *"San, san, jiu, liu, ba, yao, wu,"* *"3396815."* Eventually, the soul language arises and overrides the literal words you speak as you repeat these numbers. Do not forget the universal healing number, *"San, san, jiu, liu, ba, yao, wu."* It is very powerful.

Soul language is the language that the soul speaks. It is a tool that the soul uses to communicate with. Souls talk with each other using soul language. If you want to communicate with a higher soul or saint – Lao Tse, Buddha, Jesus, Mary, Confucius, Taoist saints, saints of other religions, your own spiritual guide, and even extra-terrestrial beings – you can do so in soul language.

Soul language is universal. It can be produced by a speaker of any language and translated into any other language. The key to understanding soul language is knowing how to translate. It can be translated into any language or dialect in the universe. If you speak English, you will interpret soul language in English. If you speak French, you will interpret in French. If you speak Chinese, soul language will come to you in Chinese. Translating soul language takes special training although some students have been able to do so in as little as a day.

When you understand soul language, you can communicate with your soul and find out if it is happy or not. What does your soul like? What does your soul dislike? Your soul will tell you. Remember that the soul's personality and characteristics are different and distinct from those of the conscious mind and the subconscious mind. You can have a happy, healthy, enjoyable life when your soul, body and mind are in harmony.

Soul language can be applied to everything you do. It can be used for prediction, business management, making business plans, reading your future; consult it for soul healing, for confirming medical conditions, for checking your potential life span.

4. How Much Power Does Your Soul Have?

How much power your soul has depends on its position in the soul world.

You can call upon your soul to help you. Most people have never talked with their soul or asked it for help. Talk with your soul. Let it know you have back pain, shoulder pain, bleeding, etc. and ask for help. Maybe, after just one request, your bleeding will stop, your migraine headache will disappear, etc.

You should also know that some people's souls will not help them. Why? Because such people are mean-spirited, jealous, and selfish. Their hearts are narrow and they have small minds. They are inconsiderate, greedy, always thinking of money or of themselves. They have not accumulated enough virtue (*Te*) through caring, compassion, love, honesty and sincerity. Even if such a person were to beg, his soul may very well say, *"Why should I help somebody like you?"* If you catch such a message from your soul, stop a moment... maybe you should change your ways.

Soul healing is very powerful, but the capacity of your soul may not be developed enough for you to get better in just one try. You may experience only a 10% improvement after one or two treatments. Then, by chance, you do something good such as helping somebody or being generous to someone in need. The next time you ask for healing, you find yourself 30% better. Maybe a few days or a few months later, you are 70% better. Soul healing can be very fast. Sometimes a single request can heal you completely. Sometimes results can be felt in just seconds. Remember to say *thank you* for all healing from your soul.

How much power your soul has depends on *Te*, the record of your virtue, which includes the *Te* you accumulate in your present life, the *Te* you have accumulated in your past lives, and the *Te* passed down to you from your ancestors.

The Tao describes it this way: *"In this life, we plant a tree; in the next life, we enjoy its shade."*

II. *Te* (Food For the Soul)

Our physical body needs three basic materials to survive – food, water, and air. What is food for the soul? Does the soul need food or not? Yes, it does. If you want to develop your soul, you must nourish it. The soul needs special food known as *Te*.

Te, pronounced *"duh,"* is the record of your deeds, both good and bad. *Te* defines the richness of your soul. *Te* is present in everything that you do. Your every action and thought form part of your current record in the universe, for better or worse. For example, good *Te* is the record of your virtuous deeds and of the care, love, compassion, honesty and sincerity with which you have shaped your existence. At the end of this life, all your good and bad deeds are tallied to determine how you will return in the next life.

There are two types of *Te*. *Yang Te* is defined as the *Te* that arises from actions that others are aware of. Sometimes you or others will tell or let be known to others what you have done. *Yin Te* describes the *Te* that arises from your unheralded actions: you helped when you saw a need and felt no need to tell others of your actions. Both *Yang Te* and *Yin Te* raise your level of *Te* in the soul world, but *Yin Te* is more powerful.

The more good things you do, the more good *Te* you accumulate. The more good *Te* you have, the more you are favoured by the soul world, the more extraordinary functions and powers you will receive, and the higher will be your accuracy in interpreting messages from the soul world.

You can increase your level of *Te* by living every day with compassion and humility. Be kind and generous. Love unconditionally. Be sincere and honest. Help and care for others. Give of yourself. Work hard. Contribute. Don't be selfish. Respect the good in your family, friends, masters, and every living thing. Live in such a way that you increase your *Te* and your spirituality.

Everything you do which is appreciated by others increases your *Te*. When others appreciate you, this feeling is reflected back to you, and nourishes your soul. The more appreciation comes your way, the more *Te* you accumulate.

Similarly, anything that you do which hurts someone also comes back to you and reduces your *Te*. Do not engage in malicious thoughts or wishes, yelling at people, or consciously hurting others. Selfishness, greediness, or any action on your part that impacts negatively on someone or something else will lessen your *Te*.

If you have done something wrong, apologize and change your behaviour. Good deeds will not erase the record of bad deeds, but they will help to raise your final level of *Te* at life's end. Try to be a better parent, stop abusing or using people, listen to what your loved ones say, empathize, help someone who is sick, do volunteer work, etc. Such acts will develop your soul by increasing your good *Te*. Everyone has the potential to improve their soul.

14

If your soul is nourished by your *Te*, then it develops and grows very fast. Your soul can be seen inside your body by people who have developed their Third Eye. If the soul is big and strong inside your body, that means your soul is nourished by good *Te* and virtue. If your soul is small and weak, this means your *Te* and virtue are low.

The level of your *Te* determines your ability to accurately receive messages from the soul world. The soul world does not help people with bad personalities or low *Te* to develop their powers. Conversely, many virtuous people are not developed because they are unaware of the techniques for development and communication, because they are not aware of the soul world, or because they do not want to interact with the soul world. Once they learn the proper techniques, however, they can develop very quickly.

Te and virtue, fighting your selfishness – these are the keys to improving the quality of your life. Honesty and sincerity are the means for increasing *Te*. When you increase your *Te*, the capabilities of your soul increase, as well as those of your physical body and your mind. Your life can be prolonged, you will enjoy better health, and you can apply your increased capabilities in everything that you do.

What then is food for the soul? If we talk about soul development, the food of the soul is good *Te*. Both good and bad deeds are recorded and tallied in the journal of your *Te* in the universe.

1. Principles To Follow

Honesty Honesty and sincerity are most important for *Te*. Never lie to the soul world.

Do Not Yell At People Yelling or swearing at people brings down your *Te*. When you yell at somebody, their soul knows it and will not be happy. They return your bad energy to you.

Do Not Think Bad Thoughts Do not wish ill fortune on anybody.

Do Not Complain Complaining drains your *Te* and decreases your luck. Instead of complaining, do kind acts and try to help others. Determine why things are happening to cause you to complain, and try to improve or rectify those conditions.

Fight Your Selfishness If you can help, do it willingly and pleasantly. If you commit yourself, follow through. Always think of others and how you can help them. Be sincere and honest. Treat others with compassion. Contribute your skills and knowledge. Do not be jealous or mean-spirited. Be generous. Love unconditionally.

One kind word unlocks many doors.

2. *Te* and Higher Saints

Higher saints are those saints and souls in heaven who have made great contributions to the world, who have accumulated much *Te* and whom the soul world has deemed worthy of the designation. Some may be people that you know; others are great saints like Lao Tse, Buddha, Jesus, Mary, Confucius, etc.

17

When you ask your own soul to help you, it may or may not respond. Similarly, when you ask higher souls or saints to help, they may or may not come to you. You may need more training or need to accumulate more *Te* before you can connect with the higher souls.

Some people pray and pray, give money to charity and kneel until their knees bleed, but if their virtue and *Te* are not high enough, the higher saints will not come to help. You lose the benefit of their immeasurable power if you are mean, selfish, greedy or inconsiderate. If your heart does not move them, the saints will not answer you.

When your *Te* has reached a certain level, you may be surprised to find that higher saints help you on request. It means they have started listening to you. Depending on your level of *Te*, even the greatest saints will come to help you.

If the saints give you special powers, know that it is because you have good *Te* and a responsibility to contribute to the world. If you don't contribute or if your personality changes and you become mean, jealous or selfish, your special gifts will be taken away. You will continue to develop much faster as long as you commit, contribute, work hard, accumulate your *Te*, and do what you can to help. These are the keys to enlightenment and accessing the powers of the higher saints and the soul world.

3. Ancestral *Te* and Past Life *Te*

Besides the *Te* that you accumulate yourself in your present life, there are two other sources of *Te* that determine your position in the soul world. One is the *Te* that you have accumulated during your past lives. The other is the *Te* you have inherited from your ancestors.

If your ancestors were good and kind, their good *Te* comes to you and to their other descendants. You will develop much faster. Be grateful and appreciate the generations before you. Their good deeds are now helping you in your life, health and business. They support you because they love you and care for you, just as you care for your children and grandchildren. Your good *Te* comes in part from the generations before you and extends to those after you.

Meditate and pray on the birthdays of your ancestors. Any requests or messages you send on these days are very strong. Ask the souls of your ancestors to communicate with you and help you. However, if your ancestors were not virtuous, do not ask them for help.

The *Te* accumulated by your soul in its past lives is also important. What did you do in your past life? What about the life before the last life? Did you accumulate good *Te* or not? You may have been a very good or very bad person in a past life, and a better or worse person in another life, but you can become a much better person in this one.

20

The universe is ruled by the principle of Yin/Yang, that of opposites, where everything changes constantly – from one thing into its opposite. Good people can become bad, and bad people can become good. This is an important theory to remember. You can change your personal situation in the world. It is up to you whether you want to improve yourself and accumulate good *Te*. Some people develop faster than others, based on a combination of past life, present life and inherited factors.

4. Money Versus *Te*

What is money compared to health? How many people do you know who have only a few more months or years to live? To them, money is nothing. What is ten, twenty, thirty more years of life worth?

Making money by gambling, cheating or using people decreases your **21** virtue. Later on, you may start to get very sick. When cancer, pain, and ulcers develop, you will consult the best specialists and try to buy back your health. But what is money compared to health? Accumulate good *Te*, not money. The more good *Te* you have, the more health you have. When you have good *Te*, you have everything.

Money does not come to those who are constantly seeking it. They should pay attention instead to finding out how they could best serve the world. If you care about your family and friends and about helping others, you will not lack for money.

What is money worth compared to the knowledge that you get from the soul world and the help you receive from the higher saints? When your life ends, your money does not follow you, but your *Te* does. Your *Te* will determine the circumstances of your coming life. What is more important – money or *Te*?

III. The soul world

Many questions beg to be asked. And answered. Do heaven and hell exist? Do souls go to heaven? Do they go to hell? Do souls die or not? Where does the soul go when the physical body dies? How do new souls begin their existence? What are old souls? How does the soul world work? Is there a next life?

All the souls in the universe, living and inanimate, form the soul world. These include new souls, old souls, good and bad souls. There are souls and saints at all different levels of enlightenment.

When does the soul come into the body? On a biological level, a woman's egg and a man's sperm each have their own souls. At the moment of conception, these merge and form the embryo's soul, which grows and becomes the foetus' soul.

When a baby is born, the human soul enters the baby's body and the foetus' soul leaves. Approximately 95% of human souls enter through the fontanel, the soft spot on the crown of the baby's head; the other 5% can enter through any other part of the body. The soul of the foetus that has left the baby's body becomes a new soul after a time.

The soul world determines when a soul will return to earth and under what circumstances. Each soul can choose the family and body that it will grow up in subject to soul world approval. At death, the soul leaves the body in the same way that it came in. The soul world again decides where it will go.

Souls can divide into many soul entities. Think of the Buddha and Jesus, who appear and offer solace to millions of people all over the world at the same time. They each have only one soul, but each can be in many places at once. They can divide and subdivide their souls to reach as many people as request their presence at any one time, anywhere.

23

Your soul can also be in more than one place at one time, performing many functions. Sometimes it visits and helps other people in their dreams or in your dreams, sometimes it travels to gain knowledge, to absorb natural energy, or to communicate with other souls. You may not be aware of your soul's activities, but the universe keeps a record of all such occurrences.

You are here for a special reason. There is a plan for your life. The soul world directs you. The soul world protects you when wars threaten, when accidents are pending, and during the critical moments in your life. If you have a connection with higher saints, they can protect you in a second from harm. The saints help to protect you and your loved ones.

1. Higher Souls and Their Powers

The soul world has a definite hierarchy and structure. Everything is relative. Whatever position your soul has obtained in the soul world, there are always souls at a higher level than yours. Higher souls are saints and souls who have reached a certain level in the soul world. Lao Tse, Buddha, Jesus, Mary and Confucius are all examples of higher souls.

You too can become a higher soul if you commit yourself to do so and contribute throughout this lifetime. Teach and benefit people in everything you do. All your contributions help you to accumulate good *Te* and elevate your standing. There are many levels in the soul world. Which level your soul belongs to depends on how much you contribute to the world. Living persons can have a very high position in the soul world. You can reach the Buddha's level and become a living Buddha.

Position is very important in the soul world. Souls in lower positions must listen to souls in higher positions. Souls in higher positions direct those in lower positions. Even when you have reached the saint level, you must respect and obey the higher saints; lower saints must listen to and obey you. Your soul can continue reaching higher and higher towards heaven. Heaven has endless levels and each of these has many sub-levels. The highest level is known as *"wu chi,"*, nothingness, Tao or God.

24

Can we communicate with higher souls? Yes. This is the ultimate purpose of soul study. Higher souls also want to find people to connect with. Communication is a two-way street, but to communicate, you must know the techniques and you must have enough good *Te*.

Communicating with higher souls is invaluable. They have inestimable powers. They will guide you, help you, nourish you, protect you, improve you and enlighten you, whether you realize they are there or not. If you have a connection with the saints and higher souls, you are protected anywhere and everywhere. They can heal you, protect you from car accidents, rescue your business, etc. The higher the saints connected with you, the greater protection you have.

Your saint connections do not stay with you all the time, but they are always there when you need them or request their assistance. They come unsummoned to protect you at critical moments. When they help you, show proper appreciation, respect and acknowledgment. Say *"Thank you!"* Saints and souls communicate with each other or anyone they wish to speak with, anywhere in the world.

The relationship between your soul, your physical body and the saints connected with you is illustrated by the concepts of *"wu chi"* and *"tai chi."* In **Figure 1**, the *"wu chi"* symbol of nothingness (on the left) repre-

sents the soul; and the *"tai chi"* symbol of Yin/Yang balance (on the right)
represents the physical body. The *"wu chi"* glyph in the middle represents the saints connected with you.

Figure 1.
The Relationship Between the Souls and the Physical Body

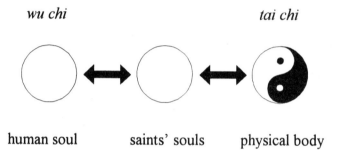

wu chi   *tai chi*

human soul   saints' souls   physical body

In the universe, Yin/Yang is interchangeable and interrelated, as are
"wu chi" and *"tai chi."* Everything in the universe can be said to be in a
state of *"wu chi"* transforming into *"tai chi"* (nothing transforming into
something), and *"tai chi"* transforming back into *"wu chi"* (something
transforming into nothing). Taoists understand *"wu chi"* to be *"wu wei"*
(to do nothing); and *"tai chi"* to be *"you wei"* (to do something). Buddhists think of *"wu chi"* as *"ding li"* (emptiness and nothingness), and
"tai chi" as *"hui li"* (intelligence and stability).

2. Your Group Head

The first saint that communicates with you is generally the group head of all the saints that will be connected with you. All other saints that come to you later do so under the direction of the group head and must obey the group head, even if they are greater. The group head arranges everything that comes to you.

27

There are many group heads in the universe, but each person has only one. You are in a very special position if you have a very high spiritual guide as your group head. The higher your group head is, the more saints are connected with him and the more power he has. Pray to your group head before any other saint. This shows the highest respect.

3. Religion In the soul world

Religious differences do not exist in the soul world. Each religion has its own theory and version of the afterlife. Buddhists think one way, Christians another, Jews another, etc. Each group has its own beliefs and philosophies. However, regardless of which group you belong to or what you believe in, there are no religious distinctions in the soul world.

For example, in the East, Tao is the highest level in heaven. *"The Tao produces One, One produces Two, Two produces Three, and Three produces all things."* In the West, it is said that God produces everything. Are the Chinese Tao and the western God the same? Yes, exactly the same. Different beliefs, but the same thing.

Pray to whomever you believe in. Pray consistently and regularly all throughout your life. The soul of Lao Tse, Buddha, Jesus, Mary, Confucius, or whoever your spiritual guide is, can come to you. Who comes depends on your faith or religion, but at the highest levels in the soul world, there is no distinction between faiths.

The structure of the soul world is based on levels only, and it is very clear who is high and who is low. Lower saints must obey higher saints.

4. Soul Judgment

Almost every religion has a version of heaven and hell. There is definitely a heaven and a hell in the soul world.

At a baby's birth, the soul world decides which soul will occupy the new body. Similarly, at life's end, the soul world decides where the soul is to go. The soul world applies this practice throughout the universe and across all religions.

Not all souls are good. Souls can be good or bad. It depends on what they like to do and also on their personalities. The soul does not die, but passes from one life to another to another. With every life, the soul undergoes a personality change.

The soul world knows everything that happens. Higher souls and the universe decide whether your soul is good or bad based on the qualities you have developed. When you die, the soul world arranges where your soul will go depending on what you have done in this life. If you did great things, served the people and served the world, your soul goes to a better place.

If you behaved very badly, you will go to hell. Praying for deliverance just before life ends helps a bit, but does not alter the judgment that the soul world passes on your soul. You go to hell to feel remorse and to atone for your mistakes. Your soul must change its personality and attitude before it can leave hell and you must make a formal request to do so. The soul world then decides whether you have changed enough to return to earth. There is no time limit to your stay in hell. Some souls stay for thousands of years until they are ready to come back.

When you have reached saint level, your soul goes to heaven. Of the many saints in heaven, some will return to earth, some will not. If the soul world thinks that the world needs help, it will send you to earth even if you did not plan to go.

Souls come back at different times, to different spaces and places. Highly developed living saints may come back instantly. Some people may take a few years, some people may take a couple of generations, others take hundreds or thousands of years before they take up their next life. In this life, your daughter or son from a previous life can be much older than you. Your past life children can come back to earth earlier than you.

The soul world decides everything.

Chapter Two

Techniques for Soul Development and Communication

35

Some people have very good *Te*. Throughout their lives they have helped many people and contributed to the world. Their level of *Te* is very high, but they can still be very sick. Why do they continue to suffer despite their great contribution to society? One of the important reasons is that they do not know how to talk with their souls and ask for soul healing.

To begin the process of communication with the soul world, you must first develop your vital energy and learn the correct techniques to open the door to your message centre. How long this process takes depends on your commitment to making it happen and on how much you practice. However, you cannot force development; let it happen naturally. The more you want this communication to happen, the longer it will take.

I. Chanting "3396815," the Zhi Neng Medicine Number

Chanting has been used for centuries for various purposes. Some chants have evolved into a sequence of voiced sounds with no discernible meaning, but these mantras are not only a sequence of sounds: they contain special messages. Many religions use such chants to connect with the universe and higher powers.

Zhi Neng medicine uses a very powerful mantram for universal healing. The number *"3396815"* is shown and explained in **Table 1**. Repeating silently or aloud in Mandarin Chinese[1] the sounds that make up this number, *"San, san, jiu, liu, ba, yao, wu,"* stimulates various internal organs, helps balance and develop energy in the body, and sends out a positive message, all at the same time.

---

[1] The Mandarin Chinese pronunciation of the numbers and healing sounds used in Zhi Neng medicine works best for healing and energy development as described. Since the message is associated with the numbers, saying them in another language still sends a healing message to stimulate the same organs, but the Mandarin version is more effective because of the vibrational quality of its sounds.

Table 1. The Zhi Neng Medicine Healing Number 3396815

Number	Mandarin Pronunciation	Area Stimulated
3	san	chest
3	san	chest
9	jiu	lower abdomen
6	liu	ribs
8	ba	navel
1	yao	head
5	wu	stomach

This mantram can be repeated while you are standing, but it is more powerful if you repeat it when you are sitting in the proper position for meditation. *"San, san, jiu, liu, ba, yao, wu"* can be repeated slowly, rapidly, quietly or loudly, anywhere, anytime. Repeating *"San, san, jiu, liu, ba, yao, wu"* is the key to higher energy development and to opening the body's message centre.

You each have your own saint guides and you can call on them when you are saying this special mantram. Ask your saint guides for answers to personal questions, for predictions on upcoming events, for healing for yourself and for others. Be specific. Be sincere and honest. Never ask for things that can harm or hinder someone else.

For example, say *"San, san, jiu, liu, ba, yao, wu. San, san, jiu, liu, ba, yao, wu. San, san, jiu, liu, ba, yao, wu. Soul world and saint guides, please give me your support. Please nourish me and give me knowledge. Please answer this question for me. (Ask your question..............) I appreciate your support. Thank you very much."* After you have opened the door to your message centre, you will be able to communicate directly with your soul and the soul world.

II. Developing Energy

Very high energy is needed for soul development. Your body must be strong enough to support the demands made upon it, and physically conditioned to be able to withstand the changes that will happen.

One of the Zhi Neng medicine techniques for developing energy is the practice of meditation in the form of creative visualization using sitting-style *Dong Yi Gong* exercises. Generally speaking, there are two kinds of meditation – the open style and the closed style of visualization.

The *Open Style of Visualization* involves closing your eyes and visualizing scenes from nature or things that are external to your body. For example, you might visualize the sun, the moon, galloping horses, waterfalls, the pyramids in Egypt, etc. When you switch quickly from image to image, your brain cells start to vibrate at a higher than normal frequency. Switching scenes even faster will help to raise the vibrational frequency even more in your cells, and this is a very powerful way to develop energy. The open style of meditation is very flexible because the range of images you can use is endless.

The *Closed Style of Visualization* involves visualizing only your internal organs or parts of your body. If you want to strengthen your heart, visualize a strong, clean, red heart. If you are having lung problems, visualize strong, healthy, clear lungs. In sum, visualize any part of your body that needs healing as being strong, vibrant and healthy. The closed style of meditation is very good for strengthening the body and internal organs, but it is less flexible than the open style because you visualize only parts of your body.

Zhi Neng medicine goes a step further by combining the open and closed styles of meditation in its *Dong Yi Gong* exercises. *Dong Yi Gong* is the Zhi Neng medicine style of *qi gong*, an ancient Chinese practice for developing and balancing the energies of the body, mind and soul.

When you practice *Dong Yi Gong*, your body cells are stimulated to vibrate alternately between states of high excitation (yang aspect) and calm relaxation (yin aspect). The more frequent the changes and the greater the contrast between the Yin/Yang energy states created within your body during meditation, the faster you develop. By comparison, development is much slower with other meditation styles that focus only on achieving tranquility.

With *Dong Yi Gong*, you visualize natural things inside your lower abdomen to develop the foundation energy centre known as the *Lower Dan Tian*. When you visualize something that includes movement, like

Three Dragons Playing with a Golden Pearl inside your abdomen, the cells of the internal organs start to vibrate. When your body cells are excited and vibrating quickly, energy (*qi*) radiates from them to strengthen the surrounding organs and also to develop potential cells in the brain[2]. This helps to make the body more sensitive and open to receiving messages from the universe through the Middle Dan Tian or message centre.

In Zhi Neng medicine, we do not encourage you to visualize images inside your *head* because this practice can cause headaches, stress, etc. With the Zhi Neng practice, you will feel very warm after doing active visualization of images inside your *lower abdomen* for about 20 minutes. This is due to the increased energy you have generated during your meditation and also due to support from the soul world.

Developing energy involves many aspects. You must have good *Te*, sincerity, good and honourable intentions, and respect for the soul world. Your physical body, the house of your soul, must also be able to withstand the training and development involved. You must know the proper techniques to use, the best times to apply them and what types of meditations work best. The key to energy development and communication with the soul world is chanting *"3396815"* or *"San, san, jiu, liu, ba, yao, wu."*

41

---

[2] Generally speaking, we use about 10 - 15% only of our brain cells. Highly developing the latent brain cells brings out functions such as telepathy, Third Eye abilities, etc.

1. Zhi Neng Medicine (The Book)

Reading the book, *Zhi Neng Medicine, Revolutionary Self-Healing Methods from China* is a very powerful way to develop your energy and power. It gives you the foundation of Zhi Neng medicine and the basis from which to better do soul study.

Zhi Neng Medicine is not an ordinary book. It is a message book. The voices of many saints and Master Zhi Chen Guo, the founder of Zhi Neng Medicine, speak through it. Read the book every day, from beginning to end. Every time you read this book, you will understand different things, and the more you read, the higher will be your level of understanding. Soon you will start reading the messages and meanings between the words. You will start to read the book within the book and see the picture within the picture.

Be relaxed when you read. Using the Zhi Neng medicine postures for sitting-style *Dong Yi Gong* is especially conducive to receiving energy and messages. Read every page to get an understanding of how powerful Zhi Neng medicine is. Reading this book is an excellent form of *qi gong* because you use your mind. Pay special attention to the energy development techniques in the second chapter. Practice *Dong Yi Gong* – the horses, the dragons, the golden ball. Do the meditations. Repeat often, "*San, san, jiu, liu, ba, yao, wu.*"

2. Best Times For Meditation

The Eastern principle of Yin/Yang applies to everything in the universe. Daytime is yang, nighttime is yin. The sun is yang, the moon is yin.
Yin/Yang theory also applies to the body, where some parts are yin and
others yang. Meditating during the times when Yin/Yang energies are
changing from one into the other helps you to develop much faster.

43

For example, yin energy is greatest and yang energy least from 11 p.m.
to 1 a.m. From midnight on, yang starts to increase and yin decreases.
Yang is highest and yin is lowest from 11 a.m. to 1 p.m., when the sun is
overhead. Nourishing or developing energy in the kidneys, which are yin
organs, is best done at midnight. Stand outside and watch the moon,
when yin is strongest. To nourish your yang energy, watch the sun rise
and absorb its increasing yang energy.

The last quarter of every hour is also very important as this is the time
when the Yin/Yang balance shifts. Changes in the natural environment
and weather conditions, typhoons, rain and snow almost always happen
in the last quarter of the hour.

Pay attention to the first day and the fifteenth day of each Chinese calendar month. These are the days of the new and full moon. Practicing *qi gong* or meditating on these days is very special and will have strong results.

In summary, if you have only a short period of time to meditate or do *qi gong* exercises, the best time is from 11:00 p.m. to 1:00 a.m. or from 11:00 a.m. to 1:00 p.m. If you have only fifteen minutes, meditate or do *qi gong* during the last quarter of any hour (e.g. 7:45-8:00). Results from meditation and energy development can be increased tenfold when you practice during these times.

3. The Body's Five Important Energy Centres

All parts of the body must be strengthened for it to support the proc-ess of soul development. Messages from the universe enter through the Middle Dan Tian, the message centre, but this is only one of the energy centres of your body. All the other energy centres must also be devel-oped and strong for optimal soul world communication.

The physical body is like a house. It is the vessel of the soul. You have a responsibility to your soul to nourish your physical body, to take care of it and to maintain its good health. Your soul lives in this house of yours. If the body becomes too damaged or too sick, your soul will have to leave, so take good care of your body. Provide a strong and worthy envi-ronment for your soul.

Think of the body as a small universe in the big universe of the world. There are five important energy centres in the body. If you pay attention to only one (e.g. the message centre), the other areas suffer neglect and remain under-developed. You must develop all areas equally to fully con-nect with the universe.

If the body's cells are not sufficiently stimulated, they will not vibrate enough to become sensitive to receiving messages from the universe. You might receive an incomplete picture or message. The more developed are the cells in every part of your body, the more sensitive they are and the more accurate your translation of the message.

Figure 2. Five Important Energy Centres in the Body

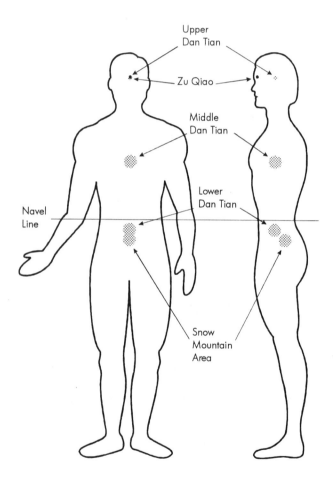

3
3
9
6
8
1
5

Zhi Neng focuses on developing energy in the five most important energy areas of the body, as shown in **Figure 2**. The five energy centres which are key to developing greater capabilities of the mind and body are:

a) the Lower Dan Tian

b) the Middle Dan Tian

c) the Upper Dan Tian

d) the Zu Qiao

e) the Snow Mountain Area.

To locate the five Zhi Neng medicine energy centres in your body, you can use the personal body inch of traditional Chinese medicine, referred to as *cun*, and pronounced *"tsun."* To find your personal inch measurement, bend your middle finger, and observe the two creases on either side of the middle joint. One *cun* is defined as the distance from the top end of one crease to the top end of the other crease (not the joint length). One *cun* is also the width of the top joint of your thumb at its widest part.

a) Lower Dan Tian

The Lower Dan Tian is a fist-sized energy centre located about 1.5 *cun* below the navel and 2.5 *cun* inside the body. Zhi Neng medicine regards the Lower Dan Tian as the energy foundation area of the body, the storehouse of its energy. The Lower Dan Tian is also the area of the body where the soul normally resides.

b) Middle Dan Tian

The Middle Dan Tian is also a fist-sized area, the middle of which is located 2.5 *cun* inside the body, starting from a point midway between the nipples. This is the message centre of the body. The Middle Dan Tian is your key to communicating with the universe. Developing the message centre is essential for developing your soul language, your intuition and your telepathic powers.

c) Upper Dan Tian

The Upper Dan Tian is a cherry-sized area located 3 *cun* below the Bai Hui, (pronounced *"by way"*) acupuncture point. The Bai Hui is located at the intersection of a line drawn from the tip of your nose up to the back of the head and a line drawn from the top of one ear, up over the head, to the top of the other ear. In western medicine, the Upper Dan Tian is the area of the pineal gland. Taoists refer to this area as the Ni Wan Gong. Buddhists refer to it as the Third Eye. Developing the Upper Dan Tian is crucial to developing greater intelligence and capabilities of the mind.

d) Zu Qiao

The Zu Qiao, pronounced *"ju chow,"* is a cherry-sized area found just inside the bone cavity behind the Yin Tang acupuncture point (midpoint between the eyebrows). The Zu Qiao is similar in function to the Upper Dan Tian.

e) Snow Mountain Area

The Snow Mountain Area is found by drawing an imaginary, horizontal line straight through from the navel to the small of the back. From the back at the Ming Men (Life Gate) point, go in one third of this distance and down 2.5 *cun* (just in front of the spinal column). The Snow Mountain Area is the most important energy area of the body, because the four most important meridians (the Ren, Du, Dai and Chong meridians) meet in this area. It gets its name from Buddhists who visualize a snow-covered mountain there.

III. Key Techniques

Zhi Neng medicine uses three key techniques simultaneously to develop energy in the mind, body and soul. Hand positions are used to create and induce fields of different intensities in the body. Sound power is used to stimulate the cells in the body to vibrate faster. Creative visualization trains the mind to concentrate and perform mental gymnastics in ways it may not be used to, and stimulates potential brain cells in the process. All three techniques are used at the same time in *Dong Yi Gong* to reinforce their effect on cell stimulation.

1. Hand Postures

There are many hand postures in meditation and Buddhist practice. Different finger positions develop energy in different parts of the body. The positions connect different meridians for proper energy flow and development. The finger positions are generally used in seated meditation posture. The fingertips do not usually touch. The following is a brief description of the most common hand postures and finger positions used in energy development.

a) *Finger Position I* The hands are relaxed and resting on the knees with the palms facing upwards. The fingers are slightly curved with the thumb and middle finger pointing to each other. This position develops the Upper Dan Tian.

b) *Finger Position II* A variation on the first hand position is to point the thumb, index and middle fingers towards each other. The thumb should be pointing between the index and middle fingers. The palms still face up and the hands are relaxed and natural, resting on the knees. This position is used for developing energy in the Snow Mountain Area.

c) *Opening Position* Both hands face palms up, with the right hand above the belly button and the left hand below the belly button. The distance between the hands is about one hand-length and the hands do not touch the body. This position is used to begin standing-style *Dong Yi Gong* exercises and it develops energy in the Lower, Middle, and Upper Dan Tian areas.

d) *Special Zhi Neng Medicine Hand Position* Close the right hand over the left thumb and make a fist. Close the fingers of the left hand over the right hand and rest the underside of both hands against the lower abdomen. This hand position is important for developing energy, for healing, and for communicating with the soul world.

e) *Prayer Position* The palms of both hands are brought up, facing each other and almost touching, in front of the chest. The palms, fingers and wrists are relaxed and natural. This position is used for developing energy in the Middle Dan Tian, the message centre of the body. It is also used for stimulating and strengthening the organs. Most importantly, this hand position is used for praying, showing respect and communicating with the soul world.

f) *Lotus Face Position* Start with the hands in the *Prayer Position*. Bring them higher and open the palms to frame the face, blossoming like a lotus flower. The base of the palms are a few inches below the chin and slightly apart. The hands are relaxed and do not touch the face. Use this position for developing intelligence and stimulating the mind. DO NOT use this position if you have high blood pressure, migraines or headaches.

g) *One Hand Near, One Hand Far Position* The near hand is 4"-8" (10-20 cm) from the body; the far hand is 12"-18" (30-50 cm) away. The palms of both hands face the body. Their relative distances from the body create fields of different intensities. This hand position is used for transferring energy between parts of the body, and for balancing or healing purposes, as well as for energy development.

Hand postures for Sitting-Style Dong Yi Gong exercises.

Cross-legged/Prayer Position (e)

Half-lotus/Finger Position II (b)

Full-lotus/Special Zhi Neng
Medicine Hand Position (d)

Detail - Finger Position II
(b)

2. Sound Power

Sound carries energy, and sound energy stimulates cells in the body to vibrate faster. The faster you repeat the sound, the more you stimulate the body. In Zhi Neng medicine, specific numbers and sounds are used to stimulate specific organs in the body. They are very powerful and they allow you to develop energy very quickly. Repeat these sounds slowly, rapidly, quietly or loudly. Saying them rapidly stimulates the cells in your body to vibrate faster. Saying them loudly stimulates the larger cells in the body; saying them quietly develops the smaller cells.

In Zhi Neng medicine, the healing numbers and sounds are said in Mandarin Chinese. Saying the numbers in another language will also result in healing because the message is in the numbers. However, the healing is more effective with the Chinese sounds because of their vibrational quality. For this reason, you will find, throughout the text, examples of how to pronounce them.

54

3. Mind Power

Along with the use of specific postures and sounds, Zhi Neng medicine includes *creative visualization* as part of its *Dong Yi Gong* practices to develop higher and more powerful energy in the mind. Training the brain with imaging and creative visualization techniques will awaken more of its cells, thereby increasing and improving mental capacity. Creative visualization is more powerful than logical thinking because it is open-ended. Therefore, use creative visualization when you meditate to speed up the development of your mind and body.

You can also develop energy very fast by visualizing bright light in your energy centres. Try to visualize bright white or golden shining light. The brighter the light, the faster you will develop. If you have difficulty visualizing, persist. It takes time to develop this skill.

IV. Developing Energy with Standing-Style *Dong Yi Gong*

The three techniques of hand power, sound power, and creative visualization are used together in the following standing-style *Dong Yi Gong* exercises to develop the five main energy centres of the body. Repeat them as often as you like.

Remember to:

- Aim the palms at an energy centre when using a *One Hand Near, One Hand Far* hand position. Both palms must face the body; do not point your hands downwards or away from the body. (If a different hand position is to be used, it will be specified.)
- Repeat the sounds out loud (or silently) as fast as you can.
- Concentrate on visualizing light flowing in these energy centres.
- Be creative. Use your imagination to make the exercises work for you.

1. Lower Dan Tian

Developing energy in the Lower Dan Tian will help to alleviate indigestion, constipation, and pain in the lower abdomen, as well as menstrual pain, weak kidneys, weak legs, etc.

- **Hands**: *One Hand Near, One Hand Far* facing the lower abdomen. **57**
- **Sound**: Repeat the sound *"hong, hong, hong"* or the number 9, *"jiu,"* pronounced *"Jew"* or *"Joe."*
- **Visualize** an electric light bulb inside the Lower Dan Tian. Imagine it burning at 40 watts, 60 watts, 100 watts, 500 watts, brighter and brighter. See it burning at 1,000 watts. Visualize an explosion of light in your abdomen!

2. Middle Dan Tian

Highly developing this area will allow you to communicate with and to receive messages from the universe. The more you develop your Middle Dan Tian, the more sensitive you become to intuitive and telepathic messages from the universe and the soul world.

- **Hands**: *One Hand Near, One Hand Far* facing the upper chest area. Alternatively, use the *Prayer Position*.
- **Sound**: Repeat *"ah, ah"* or *"woo, woo."*
- **Visualize** a golden ball of light inside your Middle Dan Tian. The ball is constantly radiating brilliant, clear light.

3. Upper Dan Tian

Developing this centre increases your mind power and helps to develop your Third Eye. It also benefits the memory and helps to reverse
senility.

- **Hands**: *One Hand Near, One Hand Far* facing the crown of the
head.
- **Sound**: Repeat *"wong, wong, wong."*
- **Visualize** a golden pearl in the Upper Dan Tian area. The pearl
glows constantly with a clear, bright, golden light.

4. Zu Qiao

Similar in function to the Upper Dan Tian.

- **Hands**: *One Hand Near, One Hand Far* facing the point midway between the eyebrows.
- **Sound**: Repeat *"wong"* or *"yi, yi, yi."* (*"Yi"* is the Mandarin pronounciation of the number "1.")
- **Visualize** a transparent, beautiful diamond in the Zu Qiao area, shining brilliantly, vibrating constantly, and causing the whole area to glow with a bright light.

5. Snow Mountain Area

The energy radiating from the Snow Mountain Area supports and nourishes the brain. Energy from the Snow Mountain Area goes down in
front of and enters the tail bone before moving up through the spinal
column to the brain. Developing energy in the Snow Mountain Area will
help you to overcome poor memory, quicken a slow response of the
nervous system and relieve tinnitis (ringing in the ears), etc.

- **Hands**: *One Hand Near, One Hand Far* facing the small of the back.
- **Sound**: Repeat *"hong"* or *"jiu."* (*"Jiu,"* pronounced *"Jew"* or *"Joe,"* is
  the Mandarin Chinese pronounciation for the number *"9."*)
- **Visualize** a snow-covered mountain in this area. Imagine a hot, powerful sun radiating heat and sunlight down onto the Snow Mountain, and enjoy the view. The snow on the mountain starts to melt.
  See and hear the melting snow as it turns to water. See energy
  rising in the form of steam. As the steam-energy rises, visualize it
  nourishing your internal organs and tissues and going to any area
  that needs healing.

6. Five-Minute Exercise For the Five Energy Centres

In this powerful five-minute energy development exercise, spend one minute on each energy centre. One minute of highly stimulating energy development is better than a half-hour of weak meditation. Visualize a golden, spinning ball of light or a burst of bright light and use soul language for sound power. Repeat *"San, san, jiu, liu, ba, yao, wu"* very fast. You can end with *"Hao! Hao! Hao!"* (*"Get well!"* in Mandarin) before going on to the next energy centre. Remember also to say *"Thank you."* (For a review of the *Hand Postures*, see pages 50-53.)

Lower Dan Tian: The hands are held tightly against the lower abdomen in the *Special Zhi Neng Medicine Hand Posture*.

Message Centre: The hands are held in the *Prayer Position* in front of the Middle Dan Tian.

Upper Dan Tian: The hands are held in the *Prayer Position* on the crown of the head.

Zu Qiao: The hands are held in the *Prayer Position*, with the backs of the thumbs at the midpoint between the eyebrows.

Snow Mountain Area: The hands are held against the small of the back in the *Special Zhi Neng Medicine Hand Posture*.

7. "Wong, Ah, Hong"

This exercise builds foundation energy, as well as healing and strengthening the internal organs in the Upper, Middle and Lower Dan Tian areas. *"Wong"* vibrates the head and stimulates the brain cells. *"Ah"* vibrates the chest and lungs. *"Hong"* vibrates the lower abdomen.

63

Inhale deeply. Exhale in one long breath, saying *"wong, ah, hong,"* and visualize red, white and blue lights as you lower your hands to face the corresponding energy centre. Repeat the sequence many times.

- **Hands**: *One Hand Near/One Hand Far* over the Upper Dan Tian.
  Sound: Say *"wong"* once, holding for one third of the breath.
  Visualize the whole brain glowing with clear, red light.
- **Hands**: *One Hand Near/One Hand Far* facing the Middle Dan Tian.
  Sound: Say *"ah"* once, holding it for the second third of the breath.
  Visualize your whole chest glowing with clear, white light.
- **Hands**: *One Hand Near/One Hand Far* facing the Lower Dan Tian.
  Sound: Say *"hong"* once, holding for the remaining third of the breath.
  Visualize your abdomen glowing with clear, blue light.

- Note: Instead of saying each sound once per sequence, you may repeat them quickly several times (*"wong, wong, wong; ah, ah, ah; hong, hong, hong"*).

8. Sha's Golden Healing Ball

Imagine a beautiful golden ball of glowing light. The golden ball has immeasurable healing powers. Gold light has the highest healing power. Use the golden ball to help develop your soul and physical body.

Spin the golden ball very fast in any part of your body that needs healing or energy development. Spin it in any area where there is chronic pain. Your soul can also be nourished and developed with the help of the spinning golden ball. Feel its energy warming you. Feel its power increase as you spin it faster and faster.

- **Hands**: *Special Zhi Neng Medicine Hand Posture*, hands held tightly against any one of the five energy centres or any area that needs healing or relief from pain.
- **Sound**: *"San, san, jiu, liu, ba, yao, wu"* (repeated very fast).
- **Visualize** a bright, golden ball of light stimulating the energy centre where you have placed your hands, or, conversely, spinning away the pain. **Visualize** the golden ball nourishing, strengthening, warming and healing you. Feel the pain disappear. **Visualize** the area as healthy, strong and free of problems.

V. Developing Energy with a Partner

Sitting-style *Dong Yi Gong* energy development exercises can be done with another person. Sit comfortably in the full-lotus or half-lotus position (see page 53). Alternatively, you can kneel or sit cross-legged.

1. Yin/Yang Energy Exchange   65

This powerful exercise involves the transfer and exchange of yin energy and yang energy between a woman and a man. All the internal organs are stimulated and strengthened as energy is moved in turn through each partner's body. Practice this exchange to develop energy and to heal problems in the limbs and extremities, the head and brain, the chest and heart, the digestive system, and the lower abdomen. This exercise will help heal bronchitis, lung inflammation, heart or kidney problems, inflammation of the liver, digestive problems, uterine conditions, incontinence, etc.

Both partners face each other, sitting in the lotus position or cross-legged with the knees almost touching. The man's arms are extended forward at waist level with the palms facing upwards. The woman extends her arms forward at waist level and rests her palms lightly on his.

Visualize a golden ball of light spinning through the corresponding organs as you say out loud, together, the sounds related to them. The golden ball spins clockwise as each partner receives energy; it spins counter-clockwise as energy is directed toward the other.

Inhale in one long breath when receiving energy; exhale when sending energy. The man and the woman help each other in turn by visualizing the flow of the energy as it moves back and forth between them.

1. *The man receives the woman's yin energy*:

   Breathing: He inhales, she exhales.

   Sound: *"Shiyi, yi, san, wu, ba, jiu,"* (the numbers 11, 1, 3, 5, 8, 9).

   Both visualize the golden ball of light spinning clockwise from her hands into his hands, through his arms, up to his head, down to the stomach, through the navel and into his lower abdomen.

2. *The man gives yang energy to the woman*:

   Breathing: He exhales, she inhales.

   Sound: *"Jiu, ba, wu, san, yi, shiyi,"* (the numbers 9, 8, 5, 3, 1, 11).

   Both visualize the golden ball of light spinning up and counter-clockwise from his lower abdomen, through the navel, to the stomach, to the chest, up to his head, down his arms and into his hands.

3. *The woman receives the man's yang energy*:

Breathing: She inhales, he exhales.

Sound: *"Shiyi, yi, san, wu, ba, jiu,"* (the numbers 11, 1, 3, 5, 8, 9).

Both visualize the golden ball of light spinning clockwise from his hands into her hands, through her arms, up to her head, down to the stomach, through the navel and into her lower abdomen.

4. *The woman gives yin energy to the man*:

Breathing: She exhales, he inhales.

Sound: *"Jiu, ba, wu, san, yi, shiyi,"* (the numbers 9, 8, 5, 3, 1, 11).

Both visualize the golden ball of light spinning up and counterclockwise from her lower abdomen, through her navel, to the stomach, then to the chest, up to her head, down her arms into her hands.

5. Repeat these four steps many times.

VI. Developing Energy with Sitting-Style Dong Yi Gong

Sit comfortably to do *Dong Yi Gong* creative visualization exercises. Sit in the full-lotus position or half-lotus position (see page 53). This forms a closed circuit and the energy builds as it flows in and around you. A comfortable alternative is to sit cross-legged. If you are sitting in a chair, your feet should be flat on the ground, ankles and legs not crossed. Your back should not be touching the back rest.

Relax the whole body. Hold your hands tightly in the *Special Zhi Neng Medicine Hand Posture* (see *Hand Postures,* pages 50-53). Place your hands against your lower abdomen. Touch the tip of your tongue to the upper palate to complete the energy circuit, and you are ready to begin the exercise.

Before you start, you may want to read aloud the visualization descriptions. The discussions will give you a better idea of what the exercises are meant to do. Be creative and open-minded. Let your body flow with the experiences. Do not be surprised if you feel it responding as you do these exercises. If you start laughing, crying, shaking, or experiencing a hot, cold or tingly feeling, this simply means that your body energy is changing and developing.

The following *Dong Yi Gong* sitting-style exercises are taken from the book *Zhi Neng Medicine, Revolutionary Self-Healing Methods from China*. They will help you to stimulate your potential brain cells and sensitize your body to receiving messages from the universe. Try to do these creative visualizations for at least an hour a day. It will benefit you for the rest of your life.

Begin and enjoy.

1. The Raging Sea

Visualize an ocean inside your lower abdomen.

The water is clear.

The sun is warm.

The view is gorgeous!

Breathe deeply. Feel the energy.

The tide laps gently, from left to right.

The breeze flows, swirling left to right.

Waves are lapping. The wind picks up. Dark clouds.

Waves chop – slapping. Whitecaps foam. Wind Howwwlls!

Wha! Wha! **WooOO! WhoooOSH!** WHOOSHHH!!

RAIN!!! THUNDER! LIGHTNING!! WIND !!!

WHIP! WHIP! SNAP!! CRACK! ZAP!!! ZAP!!!

TSUNAMI!! HURRICANE!!! TYPHOON!!!!

The whole ocean is churning, boiling, *raging*!!

Waves are smashing! Thunder roars!

S l o w l y **t h e w i n d** d i es

t h e r a i n t a p e r s

s k y c l e ars

quiet

calm

time

time is endless

Discussion

Close your eyes and picture the sea in your lower abdomen. Do other images fly to your mind? For example, in addition to the ocean, do you see things like a ship, a temple, dolphins at play? If the images are very clear, you are tapping into the intuitive portion of your brain, which is also used for communication with the soul world. You have gone beyond logical thinking, where the conscious mind is in control.

71

Relax and feel the energy of the ocean come to you. Feel the waves washing over you. Be a drop of ocean in a wave. Feel the power of the ocean and the warmth of the sun. The ocean nourishes you with its yin energy; the sun nourishes you with yang energy.

As the storm rises and the calm sea turns into a raging typhoon, yin decreases and yang increases. When the storm passes over and the ocean dies down, yang decreases and yin increases.

Visualizing the raging sea in your abdomen stimulates various organs, making their cells vibrate more vigorously. Cell vibration increases, radiating intense energy and generating stronger fields. This strengthens the organs and energy centres in your lower abdomen.

Repeat the exercise many times to reinforce the strong Yin/Yang contrast in this visualization.

2. Five Coloured Horses Galloping Up the Mountain

Visualize yourself on a horse on a plain with a mountain inside your

lower abdomen.

RED HORSE
On an open plain
Jump on in your RED robes
Walk counterclockwise **Walk**
Trot Trot *dinga dinga dinga*
Canter *dinga up dinga up dinga*
GALLOP towards the mountain *dinga*

GALLOP *up* the mountain *dinga dinga dinga*

higher higher faster faster faster up up up up

RED horse is SWEATING! STEAMING! PANTING!

SNORT! Whh-ee-ee! MUSCLES RIPPLE !! POWER!

GALLOP OUT ONTO THE TOP OF YOUR HEAD !!!
·

Stop
Rest a bit
Enjoy the view
Sitting on the horse
Turn your horse around
Jump back inside your head
RED horse starts walking clockwise
Trot Trot *dinga dinga dinga dinga dinga*
Canter Canter *spiraling down dinga down dinga*

GALLOP down the mountain *dinga dinga*

faster faster faster down down down *dinga dinga*

What is that you see in the distance? RED... A RED HEART!

GALLOP and DISAPPEAR INTO YOUR HEART

Discussion

This action-packed exercise develops energy in the five most impor-tant internal organs of the body.

As you ride your horse, spiraling furiously up the mountain, the energy developed in your lower abdomen radiates upwards to stimulate your brain. This increased energy causes the brain cells to vibrate more in-tensely and radiate more energy. As you ride down the mountain, this brain energy stimulates the internal organs, in turn, to increase and de-velop their energy.

Repeat the exercise riding yellow, white, blue and green horses. Wear robes of the same colour as the horses. The yellow horse will gallop counter-clockwise up the mountain, pop out of your head, stop, and race back down, clockwise, into the spleen. Coming down the mountain, the white horse disappears into the lungs, the blue horse rides into the kidneys, and the green horse rides into the liver.

The red horse strengthens the heart, the yellow horse strengthens the spleen, the white horse strengthens the lungs, the blue horse strengthens the kidneys, and the green horse strengthens the liver.

3. Three Dragons Playing With A Golden Pearl

Setting

There is a brilliant golden *Pearl* in your Lower Dan Tian
Green Dragon on the left. *Blue* Dragon on the right.
Yellow Dragon has its tail in Snow Mountain Area, body in front
of your spine, head in your brain.

Catch Pearl (the game)

Pearl jumps up and down

Green Dragon jumps! Blue Dragon jumps! *jump jump jump*
Green Dragon sucks in Pearl.
Spits out Pearl...*gold dust everywhere*
Blue Dragon *flies* after Pearl. Catches Pearl. Spits out Pearl.
Whoosh!! Green Dragon *chases. Catch Pearl! Spit out Pearl!*
Zooo o o m! Catch! Spit!!! Swoop! Faster! Suck! Spit! Suck! Spin!
What fun! Wee- ee-e! Hee-hee! Wonderful game!!

The Yellow Dragon's Ecstasy

Oops!
Pearl jumps into Yellow Dragon's tail
bump bump bump de bump up Yellow Dragon's tail
Oh joy! To have a golden peeaarrrrrl in my tail!
Wonderful! Now up my back! Squirm Squirmm m m with ecstasy...
Pearl Glows Blinding Hot! Pulse! Pulse! Pulse! Glow!!!
I feel very warm! Purrrrrr!
Ahh hh h! shiverrr r y delight !!!
Pearl is in my neck! in my mouth!
Twitch! Spasm! Shiver my bones! Ooh h h! How lovely!
Pt-too-ee!
SPIT OUT PEARL! SUCK IT IN !!! *SPIT! SUCK!*
SPIN! *Pearl spins Whhrrr rr r r r whirrrrrr weee wee*
Pop!
Back into Yellow Dragon's mouth and down his body!
Wiggle! Jiggle! Sigh! Lovely! Ahhhh!
Pop!
Pearl hops out of Yellow Dragon's tail

Catch Pearl again

Green Dragon snatches Pearl in his mouth
Mine! Let's play "Catch" again.

Discussion

The Yellow Dragon represents the *Zhong Mai*, pronounced *"jong my,"* or the Chong meridian, which is also known as the Vital Channel. In traditional Chinese medicine, this principal meridian connects and feeds all the main meridians in the body and regulates the flow of vital energy (*qi*) and blood.

The Green Dragon represents the liver; the Blue Dragon represents the kidneys. Green and Blue Dragons flying around and playing inside the lower abdomen increases the energy of the liver, kidney and other organs in that area.

The increased energy, generated by the dragons playing in the lower abdomen, flows through the *Zhong Mai* when the pearl inches its way up the Yellow Dragon's body. Developing energy in this meridian allows for the distribution of more energy to all the organs fed by the other meridians. This exercise is very powerful for developing energy and strengthening the whole body.

4. Ginseng Tree Growing On the Central Meridian

Visualize a ginseng seedling growing into a tree inside your lower abdomen.

Ginseng seedling
  In the Snow Mountain Area
Tender shoots reach up
    A trunk grows in your spine
      Young roots spread down to your feet
        Your arms are branches, your legs are main roots
          Standing sturdy, strong, rooted on fertile Earth
Ginseng tree branches grow and fill your head
  Reaching to the Sun - *warm, golden, healing light*
    Bask in the *radiance* as the Sun nourishes your leaves
      Leaves rustle music above your head, *winking* gold in the Sun
        Your many fruits feel *light* and rich in the breeze
Take energy from the Earth !
 Take energy from the Sun !
  Make life force energy !
Send glowing *energy* to all parts of your ginseng tree
  Feel the strength, the vitality, the life in your veins
    Feel *energy glowing, flowing* all through your body
      Nourish all parts from smallest root to topmost branch
All your organs are healthy, strong, and vibrant !
  Your roots are bright, shiny and clean
    Your trunk is a glowing golden stalk
      Your branches are golden vibrant limbs
        Your leaves shine gold and blinding in the Sun
          Your fruits are heavenly golden orbs of *energy*
Everything radiates light and energy
 You shake with this energy! Vibration!
    Feel *STRONG* as the Sun smiles on you
      Bend and sway with the Wind
        Rejoice in your strength
        Relax

Discussion

The Chinese aptly call ginseng the *"man root."* Ginseng roots truly look like miniature humans. *"Ginseng nourishes Qi and blood."* This is why ginseng is the most revered herb in the East.

77

This visualization is particularly powerful as you are the one growing the ginseng tree inside yourself on the *Zhong Mai* or Central Meridian. Your mind determines how big, how strong, and how powerful the tree is.

As the tree, you are rooted in Earth; energy from the Earth and the Sun flow through you, nourishing you. Feel the strength and vitality of your ginseng tree; draw upon its powerful healing properties as its energy runs through your veins and organs. Send this energy through the *Zhong Mai* to nourish and strengthen the rest of your body and organs.

5. Finding the Pearl At the Bottom of the Sea

Visualize an ocean inside your lower abdomen.

There is an ocean inside my tummy
Cool waters are clear blue silk
Smooth as glass

Look deep

Down

D
o
w
n
.
.
.
.
.

Oh!
Look!
A pearl!
A *golden* pearl!
At the bottom of the sea!
Glowing!   Pulsing!
Bright!   Golden!
Beautiful   Perfect
Shining   Pure
Strong!   Brave!
Beacon   Light
How lovely   Just to see
This little jewel!

Discussion

Concentrate on seeing the pearl at the bottom of the ocean for at least half an hour. It is radiating pure, golden light, and its beauty and energy take your breath away.

This exercise directly develops energy in the Lower Dan Tian and Snow Mountain Areas, and indirectly develops the Zu Qiao, and Upper Dan Tian (Third Eye) energy areas.

Focusing on the pearl stimulates the cells in the Snow Mountain Area, which rapidly develop intense energy. This energy radiates to the brain and helps to develop more of the potential brain cells.

Working with the Snow Mountain Area is a safe, easy and effective alternative to exercises that work directly on the Third Eye. Developing energy in the Snow Mountain Area also helps to counteract the energy drain that can happen through misuse of the Third Eye.

6. Seeing Yourself In Your Lower Abdomen

Visualize burning fires boiling a lake at the bottom of your abdomen.

Flames burn brightly at the bottom of Snow Mountain
    Leaping higher and higher
    Boiling Lake above
Your SMALL PERSON
    Sits placidly
    Calmly
    On a lotus flower
Floating in the middle of Boiling Lake
    Gases explode from the depths
    Whorls of mists tumble and roll
    Water hisses all around
YOU are serene
    Tranquil
    GLOWING!!
    Your body, your organs
    All shine brilliantly
    WHOLE
    STRONG
    HEALTHY
    Clear! Translucent! Pulsing!
YOU are serene
    Sitting on your lotus flower
    In this maelstrom of incredible energy
    Where the Universe ROARS! RUMBLES!
    The water ROILS! BOILS! SPITS!
    The flames CRACKLE!
YOU are serene

Discussion

The *I Ching* and *Five Elements Theory* are strongly represented in this visualization.

Water is yin; Fire is yang. Water represents the kidney; Fire represents the heart. Kidney/Water goes *up* to nourish the heart and gives it yin. Heart/Fire goes *down* to nourish the kidney and gives it yang.

81

The elements Water and Fire nourish, coordinate and balance each other. When Fire is burning and Water is boiling, yang and yin are both excited. Yin/Yang is most changeable at this moment.

Your SMALL PERSON sits serene in the middle of all this energy throughout the visualization. Sitting on a lotus flower has special significance and power. Visualizing your SMALL PERSON and your SMALL PERSON's organs glowing with *health, wholeness and strength* sends the same message to your mind, which can help translate it into reality in your physical body.

In essence, the SMALL PERSON seated in your lower abdomen is your soul. You can visualize anything you want for your SMALL PERSON. See yourself as strong, intelligent and successful. You are beautiful and loved. You have health and youth. Watch yourself fulfilling your dreams and desires inside your lower abdomen. Spend time on your SMALL PERSON and many of your visualizations will start coming true in your physical life as your soul, body and mind align in harmony.

7. Flashing Images Inside Your Lower Abdomen

Visualize anything you want inside your lower abdomen.

Watch ocean waves ripple in
The sun rising over the mountains blinds you
Pine trees sway overhead
82 Flowers waving madly
     The smiling face of a loved one
     Laughing children
     Swirling autumn leaves
     Rolling clouds of fog
Rushing mountain waters
Golden temples and cymbals
Leaping schools of dolphins
The sky dark with a thousand birds
Mist swirling off the ground in the early morning
     A kiss
     A puppy's joy
     The sheen of oil on a puddle
     A glance from across the room
     Your home
Rain dimpling a lake
The colour of pleasure
Coming home with your newborn child
Wheat fields under blue skies
     Dewdrops like crystals in the Sun
     Volcanoes gushing fiery lava
     A gleaming metal structure
     Ancient civilizations bustling with life
Heaven...

Discussion

Visualize anything and everything that comes to mind. See the images sharply and clearly inside your lower abdomen. Do not limit the flow of your mind. Visualize anything that you want.

Switch images and scenes as quickly as you can. Open yourself to the feelings that they bring.

Changing images quickly stimulates the brain cells to vibrate faster and develops mind power very quickly.

VII. Developing Communication with the soul world

The soul inside your body wants to talk with you. Your soul has tried communicating with you many times but does not understand that the message door to the body is blocked. Once this blockage is removed, you can communicate with your soul, the souls of other people, the souls in other things, and higher souls.

Before communication can occur, three things must happen. You must:

1. Open the door of the physical body.

2. Develop the communication tool(s).

3. Learn to translate the messages.

1. Opening the Message Centre

The message centre is also known as the Middle Dan Tian energy centre of the body. This is the door which opens onto the universe. It is closed in most people. The message centre must be fully open for you to be able to communicate with the universe.

How do you open the door? Knock first.

You have to knock on the door of the message centre located in the middle of your chest. You literally have to thump this area. The key to unlocking the door is repeating the special Zhi Neng medicine number, *"San, san, jiu, liu, ba, yao, wu,"* "3396815," while you thump your chest. As you develop, you will find that your thumping involuntarily becomes quite rapid.

In general, the procedure for opening the message centre is as follows:

1. *Develop energy in your body.*

   Practice the energy development exercises in this book and in the book, *Zhi Neng Medicine, Revolutionary Self-Healing Methods from China.*

2. *Close the hands in the Prayer Position.*

   This signifies respect for the soul. The hands are placed in front of the chest, at the midpoint between the nipples.

3. *Request assistance from the soul world.*

   Ask for help in opening the message centre. Be sincere and humble. Say *"Thank you."* You cannot open the message centre if the soul world does not support you.

4. *Repeat "San, san, jiu, liu, ba, yao, wu," "3396815," as fast as you can.*

   Say it faster and faster. This mantram is the one key for opening the message centre, developing your soul, and developing your healing powers. The different numbers vibrate different parts of the body individually and the number combination has a special message of its own. Repeating *"San, san, jiu, liu, ba, yao, wu"* is the key to your development.

5. *Thump the middle of your chest with your hands.*

This essential step is a key procedure for your development. As you repeat *"San, san, jiu, liu, ba, yao, wu,"* your thumping will become involuntary. It may even surprise you by its intensity and force, but this is a step everyone must go through. Do not be concerned about hurting yourself. If your body energy is developed, you will not feel any pain.

87

Practice these key techniques every day. Concentrate fully while saying *"San, san, jiu, liu, ba, yao, wu,"* and thumping the middle of your chest. This stimulates the cells in the message centre area to vibrate, which is the only way to open it. Some people take months or years before they develop; others take only a few minutes or days when there are higher forces helping.

2. Signs of Development

Your body will respond and give certain signs of development as you practice opening your message centre.

a) Your Soul Speaks Soul Language

Eventually, when you repeat *"San, san, jiu, liu, ba, yao, wu"* as fast as you can, a unique sound will develop in its place. You will find that you can no longer say the numbers individually and that what comes from your mouth is an involuntary sound that overrides everything else. Let this sound flow. This is the voice of your soul as it speaks *soul language.*

Each person's soul will have a different voice. Some people may speak *"babababa"* or *"namnamnamnam"* or *"loolooloo"* or some other seemingly senseless babble. The soul language is not a product of the conscious mind. Anyone can twist his tongue and generate some meaningless sound. Soul language is the special sound that comes of its own volition when you try to say *"San, san, jiu, liu, ba, yao, wu"* as fast as you can.

When you are very tired, it is easier to bring out your soul language. Practice every day for at least half an hour. One hour is better; two hours, even better. Practice saying *"San, san, jiu, liu, ba, yao, wu"* as fast as you can before you sleep and when you wake up.

You can help other people come out with their soul language by pointing at their message centre and speaking your soul language to them as they try to develop theirs. The message in your soul language and your pointing will stimulate them to develop faster.

Letting your soul speak is one thing. You must learn the *ABC's* of this new language to translate and understand what your soul is saying. Most importantly, you will learn how to apply the power of soul language in your life.

b) Higher Saints Connect With You

When your soul has reached a high level of development you may experience visitations from higher souls. For example, Jesus, the Buddha, other Buddhas or saints may visit you. Do not be afraid as they are your friends and have come to help you. Be appreciative; listen to what they have to say and obey.

Do not refuse any friends who come to you in this way or you will block important elements in your development. You cannot afford to lose the benefit of their protection and powers or the opportunities they give you. Welcome all such friends who come to you.

A saint may connect with you at the moment your body experiences lightness or involuntary shaking after you say *"San, san, jiu, liu, ba, yao, wu," "3396815."* Which saint comes depends on the spiritual leader you follow and what you believe in.

How do you know if the saints are with you or not? There will be many signs. Some people hear voices when they meditate. Others get visions. Accidents are averted. Sometimes, there are just too many incidents working in your favour for it to be a coincidence. When such things happen, ask the soul world if there is any special saint with you. Who is it? Lao Tse, Buddha, Jesus or his disciples, Mary, some saint whose name you do not know? Pay your respects to all those who come to you and thank them for being with you.

c) Your Physical Body Responds

Very few people develop their souls, bring out the soul language, and develop accurate translation abilities without experiencing various responses in their physical bodies. These reactions may include involuntary movements, pain, fatigue, crying, disturbed sleep patterns, dreaming more than usual and even improved health. These are all good signs that the body is responding to the increased energy you are developing. You will experience these things for a short time until the body adjusts itself and the message centre opens.

Some people shake, rock or jump constantly due to the high levels of energy in their bodies. Others sing, scream, laugh or cry uncontrollably. Many people cry from happiness, releasing blocked energy. Some people get very tired and sleepy and yawn uncontrollably. Others experience a tingling sensation in their bodies. Some sweat and feel as if their bodies are burning. Any such experiences are acceptable. Most of your body's responses are due to the high levels of energy it is experiencing as your soul develops.

Your body must shake uncontrollably before you can translate the soul language accurately. This develops and opens the tiniest cells in your body. If the tiny cells are stimulated, you can receive subtle message waves from the universe, which makes you more sensitive. You will be able to understand higher-level messages and translate more accurately after your body goes through this phase.

d) The Third Eye

In some people, the Third Eye may respond and start to open, allowing them, for example, to see auras when they look at other people.

An open Third Eye gives those who have developed it the ability to see things that are not normally seen within the visible light spectrum, such as auras, energies, internal organs, bones, etc., and even people's souls.

Some people have a developed Third Eye from birth or manage to develop it naturally, without effort. Others must work hard. However, concentrating on developing the Third Eye can be risky. Many people who undergo training to open it experience pain and headaches when too much energy accumulates in the brain due to incorrect training or improper practice. They may even experience some form of mental disorder. The Third Eye function develops in tandem with the other energy centres. Do not want or expect too much too soon.

Excessive use of the Third Eye function can quickly exhaust you because trying to see with it consumes a lot of the body's energy. Your five energy centres should all be highly developed and balanced to prevent physical deterioration and exhaustion. If your Snow Mountain Area is not strong, you could weaken yourself by using the Third Eye daily.

Many spiritual masters pay too much attention to the Third Eye and its functions. In Zhi Neng medicine, developing the message centre (the Middle Dan Tian) is considered to be much more important for communicating with the universe than developing the Third Eye (the Upper Dan Tian).

The ability to use the Third Eye is considered to be a lower stage of development than soul language and direct communication with the soul world. This is because the Third Eye gives you images only, whereas soul language can give you answers if you know how to communicate and translate. When you have direct communication, the answers come without your having to use the medium of soul language.

3. Exercises To Open the Message Centre

Practice any of the following exercises to open your message centre faster.

1. Have a partner stimulate your message centre by helping you thump it while speaking soul language to you. Visualize the door of the message centre opening. Your partner directs energy to your Middle Dan Tian.

2. Lay on the floor. Massage your own message centre while saying *"San, san, jiu, liu, ba, yao, wu"* to vibrate the cells there. Say it faster. Faster! End with *"Hao! Hao! Hao!"* (*"Hao!"* is Chinese for *"Get well!"*)

3. Visualize a SMALL PERSON inside your lower abdomen and use soul language to talk to him or her. Refer to the creative visualization exercise *Seeing Yourself In Your Lower Abdomen* on page 80.

4. Stand behind your partner or form a circle with several people. Touch the back of the person in front of you in the area of the message centre and repeat *"San, san, jiu, liu, ba, yao, wu"* while visualizing a golden ball of light spinning inside it. Spin the ball faster. Feel its glow. Repeat, touching the *Snow Mountain Area.*

5. Standing in a circle, request the soul world's help and have the whole group repeat *"3396815"* rapidly to assist someone in opening his or her message centre. Send your love and visualize the message centre opening as you say *"Open! Open! Open! Thank you. Hao!"*

6. Stand with a group of people packed into a very tight circle. Everyone faces out, with their hands in front of their chest in the *Prayer Position*, speaking soul language. After ten minutes or so, the group will develop very powerful energy, radiating a field of great intensity. This is known as the *Zhi Neng Beehive*.

If you are fortunate enough to be practicing with a Master:

1. Point at your Master's Middle Dan Tian. (You can also point at some other highly developed person to benefit from this exercise.) Close your eyes as you chant *"Open! Open! Open! San, san, jiu, liu, ba, yao, wu"* and see a golden ball of light spinning inside his or her message centre. Visualize the message centre opening. Try to see something, anything, inside the Master's message centre.

2. Relax as the Master requests the soul world to help you open your message centre. Assist by saying *"San, san, jiu, liu, ba, yao, wu"* as fast as you can.

VIII. Translating the soul language and Increasing Accuracy

Soul language sounds meaningless until you learn how to translate it. Once you have achieved a degree of translation, you must work on improving your accuracy. This comes gradually.

97

Follow these three guidelines to increase your accuracy in translating soul language:

1. Practice, practice, practice.

2. Increase your *Te*.

3. Show respect and say *"thank you."*

1. Translating the soul language

Once you have opened the door to communicating with the soul world, you must learn to translate the messages you receive. You must continue to practice to increase your accuracy in interpreting the soul language. There is no point in having the ability to interpret soul language if your accuracy remains low.

The key to translation is not to use your conscious mind. Let the soul world borrow your mouth to speak the message. If you interfere by trying to control the word flow or by using logic, your accuracy will not improve. You must remember that it is not you speaking – your soul and the soul world are using your mouth as a tool to communicate their messages.

The message wave from the universe comes to you through the door in your chest, the message centre. It travels from the message centre to the subconscious mind for interpretation. As your soul voice comes out, your subconscious mind relays the message to your conscious mind, which in turn listens to the voice and deciphers its meaning.

The steps that take place when you communicate with the soul world via soul language are as follows:

1. The conscious mind makes a request for information from the soul world.
2. The soul verbalizes the message using soul language.
3. The universe sends the answer to the body's message centre in the form of a message wave using soul language.
4. The message goes to the subconscious mind for interpretation.
5. The subconscious mind relays the message to the conscious mind.
6. The conscious mind directs the mouth to speak the message transmitted.

The only step in the whole process of communication that is prone to error is the transmission of the message between *Step 5* and *Step 6*, as described above. The accuracy of interpretation decreases if there is interference or an attempt by the conscious mind to shape the message. Never guess what the message is. The conscious mind must let itself be used only as a broadcaster or loudspeaker to voice the message from the soul world.

The key to translation is summed up in this one instruction: **Relax.** *Lend the mouth; do not use the brain. Let the words flow out naturally.*

Accuracy is a relative term. No matter how well you already translate soul language, you can always improve your accuracy. Sometimes, you are able to catch 90% of the message. At other times, you may be relaying only 60% of the essence. Your translation accuracy will not be consistent until you develop more fully. The accuracy of your translation also depends on your level in the soul world. You will be denied access to information if you are not qualified to receive it.

With the right instructions and guidance, some people have learned to translate soul language in one day. For many other people, bringing out this ability may take weeks, months or years. How fast you develop depends on many things. The chief factors affecting the accuracy of translation are:

1. *How much you practice these techniques.*

   Practice, practice, practice. The soul world will be patient and guide you while you are developing. Use all opportunities to practice. It is important to speak soul language as much as possible. If you can, practice translating soul language while sitting on the floor as this gives you a stronger connection to the universe.

2. *How much Te you have accumulated.*

The soul world does not help people of low virtue. Increase your translation accuracy by doing good deeds.

3. *How much you respect the soul world.*

Be humble and appreciative. Never trivialize the gifts or powers you have received from the soul world.

2. Increasing Your *Te* (Fight Your Selfishness)

How can you communicate better with the universe and the soul world? Increase your level of *Te*.

How accurately you translate soul language depends on your *Te*, the sum of your virtuous deeds. The key to increasing *Te* is to fight your selfishness and give of yourself. Stop thinking so much of yourself. Instead, think of others and of how you can help them. Be kind, compassionate, generous, loving and sincere. People who are mean, jealous, dishonest or uncaring will not be able to translate well.

Do as much as you can to contribute to the world. Use all of the talents and resources available to you. If you can help more, do so. Do not talk about doing something good and then not do it: you are judged by your actions. It is not your station in life that determines the significance of your contribution, but your heart. When you help people, do not expect any return from them. Do whatever you do with love. Do it unconditionally. Forget yourself. This is all part of *Te*.

When your *Te* is high, you will have a good life, so accumulating *Te* is much more important than accumulating wealth. You cannot take money with you when your life ends. Donate it. *Te* speaks for you in the soul world, not your money.

The Chinese have a saying, *"The mountain is easy to move, but the personality is hard to change."* Work on changing your attitude and character for the better. Discipline your temper. Be calm and more tolerant. Be kind-hearted. Respect your friends, your family and those who help you. Do not play with or use people. Be pure. Live a virtuous life where your actions and thoughts are consistent.

Sometimes, the soul world will test your character by giving you false messages. They are testing your honesty, tolerance and sincerity. If you complain, they will continue to give you more wrong messages; they may even take away your gifts and stop communicating with you. Be thankful and appreciative of anything that they give you, including what seems like wrong messages, and try to improve.

The scale of your contribution is related to your accumulation of good *Te*. Suppose you are learning a new skill. If your intention is to use this new knowledge for yourself only, it will help you in your life but you will not increase your *Te*. If you think instead, *"How am I going to use this knowledge to help my friends?"* and you start applying it, your level of *Te* rises. If you start teaching or doing volunteer work using this new knowledge, your level of *Te* rises even further. The more people you reach or touch with your contribution, the more good *Te* you accumulate. Think globally, think of your descendants, think of your next life.

The principles given here can help you achieve saint status in the soul world. If your heart is totally committed to contributing to the world, you can become a living Buddha, an earth angel, a live saint. You can reach this level and higher. Why not?

3. The Importance of Respect and Thank You

Gratitude is the key to success in everything, including increased accuracy in your translation of the soul language. Saying *"Thank you!"* should be a part of your nature. Thank all those who help you – your Master, your friends, your doctor, your lawyer, your spouse, your children, anybody who does anything for you, and especially, heaven and the higher **105** saints. Show gratitude in your actions as well as your words.

Respect and humility are very important for higher soul development. Respect is not about religion. Respect is about showing proper appreciation to those you hold in high esteem. Do this by acknowledging their significance in your life, praying to them and thanking them.

a) Respect Is Voluntary

Respect is totally voluntary. Show respect because you want to and because you know it is the right thing to do. Respect the higher saints and your spiritual leaders. Respect your Master and your teachers. Respect the friends that help you. Respect your parents. Respect all those who have helped you in the past. Respect the good in everybody and everything. Give thanks for everything in your life.

When you give respect to the higher saints, they do not expect you to promise something in return for their assistance. Some people donate large sums of money thinking that it will help their cause, but this is to no avail. Other people request special favours and receive them without promising anything in return. This is because the higher powers do not demand anything in return. However, if you have been helped, it is only proper and respectful to contribute something to show your appreciation and thanks.

Commitments are voluntary, so never promise something and then not do it. Neglecting to carry out the commitments you have made amounts to lying and lying to the soul world is a much worse offense than lying to ordinary people. Why? Because the saints know everything. Lying is disrespectful and very serious. The higher powers will respond, not by harming or punishing you, but by not looking out for you any more.

b) Small Courtesies

Respect your friends, respect your Master, and respect the heavens. Learn to show respect properly.

For example, when speaking soul language with a partner, show respect to the person you are talking with. Face each other and place your hands in the *Prayer Position*. This shows respect for each other's soul. At the same time, you are showing respect for the soul world.

When you are addressing the soul world, be serious and sincere as laughter is disrespectful. Sit in the proper posture to meditate and begin by showing respect to your spiritual guides.

Pay the highest respect to your group head, for this higher saint is the most important saint connected with you. Your group head protects you in every way, gives you luck in business, helps with your family and career, and saves you from disaster.

When you pray, start by mentioning the name of your group head and the names of the saints connected with you, if you know them, and then call upon the saints and higher souls in the soul world in general. Thank them for supporting, guiding and protecting you and ask them for their continued support and help with any special request you may have. Always say *"Thank you!"* to them and to heaven.

c) On Kneeling To the Saints

You may have your own beliefs and a creed that you follow, but feel no shame to kneel to heaven. If you do not respect heaven, you do not respect any saint or higher soul. Show respect. Kneel to your group head, to Lao Tse, Buddha, Jesus, Mary, etc.

Kneeling is a strange custom for Westerners to accept, so if you are uncomfortable with kneeling, you can show respect in other ways. However, if a higher saint requests that you kneel, is that so much to ask? You are merely showing respect.

The Chinese way of kneeling is to come from a standing position onto your hands and knees, and to bow touching your forehead to the ground several times. Bringing your head to the level of your feet shows special appreciation. Generally speaking, touching the head to the ground nine times while you are in this position signifies very high respect. There is added significance to bowing 108 times and 1,000 times. How many times you bow depends on how you feel. If you have a number of saints connected with you, acknowledge them (even the unnamed ones). Kneel and bow to them all at the same time.

There is only one rule about kneeling. Kneel to those higher than you. Lower souls and saints bow to higher ones. Kneeling is not about religion; kneeling is a mark of respect.

IX. Direct Communication

There are several ways to communicate with the soul world and the universe.

Soul language is the most common mode because for most people, it is the first step and soul language is relatively easy to bring out and develop. Afterwards, it is just a matter of translating soul language accurately. If you want an answer to your question, you must ask the soul world, which gives you the answer in soul language, at which point you can translate into any other, more meaningful language.

Another mode of communication that some people develop is *direct communication*. You can communicate directly with souls, plants, or anything else in the universe without going through soul language. Direct communication is harder to achieve than soul language and can take months or years to develop.

In one type of direct communication, an internal voice speaks directly with you, as if through a telephone. You can look at a picture and have the souls in the images speak directly with you, be they people, statues, trees, etc. You can determine if a person is of good character or not just by connecting through his or her name. In the same way, you can assess a company, know how well it is doing, and whether it will be successful or not. You can do the same thing for real estate, investments, decision X versus decision Y, etc. This is known as the *invisible telephone* function.

In a second type of direct communication, words and images are visible, as if on a television screen in front of you. This is a higher Third Eye function, which is safe to develop only after one has obtained his or her soul language. This higher ability is known as the *invisible television* function.

Developing the *invisible television* function is more difficult than developing the *invisible telephone* function. In all of China, only two or three of Master Guo's disciples have developed this skill.

Chapter Three

Applying the Power of the Soul in Your Life

115

Everything is recorded in the universe. There are no secrets at the soul level; the soul world knows everything. All of the information in the universe is open to you if you are developed enough to communicate and translate accurately through soul language. The power of the soul can be used to improve every facet of your life: it will guide you in healing, business, research, investments, communication and decision-making; it will help you to prolong and improve the quality of your life.

Soul healing, the highest form of healing in the universe, is Zhi Neng medicine on the *message* level. On the *energy* level, Zhi Neng medicine combines sound, hand and mind power to correct the body's energy imbalances. It operates at both the energy and message levels to harmonize your mind and body with your soul. This creates a healthy, joyous and nurturing environment for the spirit that is uniquely you in this lifetime.

I. Rules and Principles of the soul world

You must be serious in your interactions with the soul world. Appreciate and treasure the gifts it confers upon you. Be honest, sincere and respectful. Be mindful of your *Te*. Understand and operate within the protocol that exists.

1. Codes of Conduct

Receiving information and knowledge from the soul world is a special privilege. You have been trusted with a great gift. Treat it with the respect it deserves. You are expected to observe certain codes of conduct. Chief among them is the rule of *no disorder*: no information that you receive from the soul world should be used if it causes disruption. In general, do not request information on anything involving personal life, past life, politics, or police matters.

a) Personal Life Matters

Do not ask any questions related to someone else's personal life. It is not good *Te* for you to inquire about your girlfriend, boyfriend, spouse, business partner or anyone else. For example, do not ask how many girlfriends this man has or if your wife is unfaithful.

The answers you receive will often be incorrect if your accuracy level in translating is not yet high enough. Acting upon such information would be a mistake, and most certainly disruptive.

Alternately, the truth may come through, but it serves no good purpose for you to know it. You may have been sad before; now you become much more depressed. In essence, you are given knowledge from the soul world to make life better for you, your family, your friends and all the other people you can help, not to create disharmony.

If you are seeking clarification from the soul world on a situation that affects you personally, and you must truly know the answer, it is best to ask the question yourself. For one thing, hearing this information from other people may be more upsetting. Also, they are required to filter out any elements that would be disruptive or information that you are not qualified to know, so the answer you get may be only partial.

b) Past-Life Matters

So, you think you have found your past-life lover, sister or boyfriend! What do you do about it? *Nothing.* The rule in such matters is that you are not to cause any disorder in this life. What you had then was in a past life; this is now. You each have new families and commitments. No matter what relationship you believe you may have had with someone in a past life, do not disrupt the present lives you each lead. For example, you cannot leave your present wife and family to try to recreate what you believe you had with someone from another life.

Additionally, if you are aware of a past-life relationship with certain people, you cannot approach them about it if they are unaware of the situation. Doing so would cause disruption in their lives. You may find several close past-life companions in your present circle of friends. In fact, these people may have been close to you in several past lives. However, unless they are also aware of a past-life connection, you must keep the information confidential.

Think three times before you do anything, even if you feel very close. This is the principle.

c) Politics

Do not ask the soul world about political matters. It does not involve itself in such things. For example, it serves no purpose to ask who will become the next leader of the country, or when the election will be called.

d) Police Matters

Do not inquire about police matters or criminal investigations, unless they happen to involve family or close friends. For example, it is not your business to ascertain or report on who murdered whom. Do not get involved. The soul world knows who did what and will judge accordingly when the time comes.

II. On Having a Master

The Chinese have a saying, *"One day Master, whole life father,"* meaning that your Master is your Master for life.

The old Masters taught their disciples with a closed mouth. Many followed for a lifetime, but secrets were only given to one disciple per generation. Some Masters would not teach. Some Masters did not know how to teach. Some Masters did not have much to teach. Be grateful if you find a wise and generous Master. Treat the Master with due respect.

Always thank your Master, for the Master is the one who brings you through the door. Even if you develop beyond the Master, you are still the disciple, and you must always show respect for your Master.

If you learn Tai Chi, thank your Tai Chi Master for the gift of his teaching. If you are an artist and have learned from a special Master in a certain field, thank that Master. For any occupation, thank your mentor, thank your teachers, your professors, etc. If they had not entrusted you with their knowledge, you would not be where you are today.

Do not criticize or belittle your Master as this is a great insult to the priceless knowledge that he or she has given you. Your gifts will be diminished and heaven will rescind your powers for such disrespect.

In China, to show total respect, disciples kneel and bow nine times every time they greet their Master. This is a small but important courtesy. In the heavens and the spiritual world, bowing and kneeling are signs of respect, and they have no religious connotation. In the West, which has different customs, you can show respect to your Master by greeting him or her with your hands in the prayer position.

Always, you respect the Master, and the Master respects you.

Do not lie.

Obey your Master.

One day Master, whole life father.

The Master can teach all in one sentence.

The Master's door is open; go or stay as you wish.

Touch your Master's heart and he will give you all.

III. Applications

Knowledge of the soul can be applied to any field. The soul world will answer truthfully whether you should do this or that, whether an investment you are considering is sound, or whether a career move you are considering will be good for you. You can ask if your research is on track

or what days you should avoid air travel. You can ascertain the character of a person before you get more involved. The applications are endless, but follow the rules and principles in deciding what you may ask.

If you have benefited financially from information given to you by the soul world, it is only right that you return some part of the gain. The soul world does not mind if you charge a modest fee when you pass along information that it gives you. It understands that you have to survive. However, do not be too greedy with the fee you charge.

1. Communication

Soul communication transcends distance, time and language.

Soul communication crosses distance. When you communicate on the soul level, you can, for example, communicate with your daughter who is several thousand miles away. Use soul language to send a message like, *"I love you and I miss you."* You can also request an answer from your daughter's soul and it will respond, even if she is not consciously aware of it. Her soul knows that the communication has occurred.

Soul communication bridges time. You can also communicate with the souls of deceased people whom you have loved and those who have inspired you. It could be your grandmother, long since passed away, or a late author whose words have touched your heart. When you have developed your soul language, you can ask their souls to come and talk with you; they will not refuse. Your love draws them to you and their souls will come. If your level is high enough, you can talk to anyone you choose.

Soul communication transcends language. When you ask a question of the soul world, the answer is universally understood by anyone who has mastered the technique of soul communication. The person receiving the message can translate it into whatever language he or she speaks.

For example, a speaker uses his conscious mind to give a speech in Mandarin Chinese. Listeners who do not understand Mandarin can then ask the soul world to translate the speech into soul language. At this point, the soul language can be translated into any other language.

2. Healing

Health is the highest priority. This was recognized in China thousands of years ago, where the greatest healers were on par with the emperor.

Soul healing techniques make Zhi Neng medicine the health science of the 21st century. Basic Zhi Neng medicine uses sound, hand and mind **125** power to heal the mind, body and soul. However, these techniques may not be enough. Adding the use of soul healing, another pillar of Zhi Neng medicine, can sometimes result in almost instantaneous improvement as it is supported by the soul world.

Soul healing can also require more than one treatment. For example, people with low *Te* generally take longer to heal. Soul healing may alleviate pain and speed recovery from chronic conditions, cancer, bone fracture, coma, fibromyalgia, fatigue, depression, and other ailments. It can be used as a diagnostic tool and for preventive therapy. Use soul language to ask what is wrong with the patient. What is the true cause of the illness? What is the best treatment? The soul world will answer you.

Almost every case of physical pain is related to conflict between the soul and the mind. The conflict manifests itself in physical ailments, pain and sickness. Many illnesses occur because the soul is not happy and it responds by making the body sick.

Many things can make the soul unhappy – sexual abuse, physical abuse, stress, family pressures, strained work relations, business failures, unrequited love, etc. Souls can also carry their wounds and sadnesses from life to life, which may surface as suicidal tendencies. The root cause of depression is related to conflicts of the soul.

Your home *feng shui* could also be affecting your health. The messages and energy in your surroundings may be sending you damaging influences. For example, if you were born in the *Year of the Rat* or the *Year of the Rabbit*, do not hang any pictures of eagles or have any eagle artifacts in your home. The eagle image carries a message which could make you weak and sick.

Another example of the importance of the message factor occurs in acupuncture, where needles are used to stimulate the meridian points of the body. While some people get well from one acupuncture treatment, others take much longer. People who are afraid of the needle can block their treatment or hinder its effectiveness. The needle has a soul and receives their message that they hate needles. You will never get well with acupuncture if you resist the needle.

Recovery starts with the soul. When you want to heal yourself, telling your conscious mind to get well is not enough. Talk directly and positively with your soul as well, and ask it to help heal you. When the body, mind and soul are in balance, you will experience good health and harmony.

127

How much healing power your soul commands depends on your level of development and on your *Te*. If you have connections with the higher souls and the saints, you can also call upon them to heal both yourself and others. However, it is generally difficult to get good healing results when you try to heal someone at a higher level of soul development than yourself because that person's soul is not obligated to listen to yours.

3. Protection

Everything that happens or that will happen is known by the saints. They have inestimable powers and can grant you the benefit of their protection in times of crisis. How much you communicate with them determines how much they look out for you. The saints can save you from imminent disaster, they can snatch you back from death, they can divert you from your normal path so that you avoid a collision, etc.

Soul communication can be applied to everything you do and you can ask the soul world for answers in specific situations. For example, every morning before you drive off to work, ask if it is safe to drive. If you have an airplane to catch, check to see whether any mishaps could be connected with that particular flight number. Should you have dinner with this man? Is it all right to walk home tonight or should you take a cab? Why not check that the children will have a safe walk to school? The possibilities are endless...

4. Locating and Finding Objects

The power and knowledge of the soul world can be used to locate mine sites and ore deposits on a map. Finding the best place to sink a hole for water is another application. You can determine the extent of gas and oil reserves, you can find another coal seam, you can pinpoint the location of the next big archaeological dig, etc. If you lose something like a key or your wedding ring, you can ask for assistance in finding it.

5. Making Predictions

The power of the soul can also be applied in making general predictions and for business forecasting.

You can ask questions and get direction from the soul world about things like buying property, building a house, taking out or renewing a mortgage, etc. Should you invest money in this stock or that one? What will be the market highs and lows for today? Should you start a new business? What are the critical months? Should you start a joint venture in this particular country or not? Should the company invest research money into the development of this particular product? When will business pick up? Is this property a good investment? What crops should you plant next season?

Examples involved with the writing of this book include designing the cover with direction from heaven, deciding on the editing changes to be made, and picking the best book distributor. In setting up an office, you might use soul language to help you decide which photocopier or phone system to lease, whether to buy an IBM or a Macintosh computer system, or if a new employee is going to work out. The soul world can help you with all such decisions.

You can also ask for guidance in everyday matters. Should we vacation this month or next? Is it better to pay cash for the car or take out a loan? Is this the right school for my child? Is this plant happier in this location or that? Is this person trustworthy? Should we have another child? What should we name the baby? Soul world messages exist for everything.

6. Making Healthy, Intelligent and Beautiful Children

Developing the souls of children is very important as they have their whole lives before them. Children develop very easily and become powerful very fast.

132 Making healthy, intelligent and beautiful children starts long before conception. Such children come from parents who love each other and who have good *Te*. Conception should be avoided after one has been drinking alcohol, for children conceived at this time will be high-strung, nervous and hyperactive.

During the pregnancy, both parents should communicate with the child and give messages of love and support. Say the special Zhi Neng medicine healing number, *"San, san, jiu, liu, ba, yao, wu,"* *"3396815,"* with your hand on the woman's belly. Visualize the child as being strong, beautiful, kind, healthy and intelligent. This is one of several special exercises the mother can do before, during and after pregnancy so that the child will be born healthy and very special.

7. Increasing Longevity and Improving the Quality of Life

How long can people live? 75 years? 128 years? 250 years? Some Buddhists are said to have lived hundreds and even thousands of years. Life is endless with the Tao.

How long you live depends on yourself. How long do you want to stay **133** on this earth in this lifetime? Learn how to prolong your life by living a balanced lifestyle and by accumulating good *Te*. When you are balanced, you are healthy. Some people still enjoy life at 90 years of age; some want to live to 200; some young people are miserable and want to end their lives tomorrow.

How enjoyable can a long life be if you have serious heart problems, cancer, or arthritis? The quality of life has to be considered in relation to its length. Focus on the quality aspect first and cure your sicknesses and problems before thinking about longevity. The physical body is like a house. The soul lives inside. Look after your body well, for once the house is damaged beyond reasonable repair, the soul may decide to end the life and leave. If the soul wants to go, it will do so unless a higher soul intervenes. Tend well your soul for if it gets sick, the physical body will suffer and start ailing.

Practice the following techniques to prolong your life and stay younger and healthier. Think younger. Communicate with your soul. Do exercises to balance your energy. Develop energy to make your physical body stronger. In particular, concentrate on creative visualization exercises, such as seeing a baby or a young child as the SMALL PERSON inside your lower abdomen. At the same time, work on increasing your *Te* by helping as many people as you can and by serving the world. Accumulating *Te* is the single most important factor in prolonging your life. Doing these things will make you feel healthier, more energetic, more alert and younger!

Conclusion

The science of soul study is a part of Zhi Neng medicine that defies comprehension by most people. I have attempted to give you, the reader, an overview of knowledge concerning the soul that has been hidden for thousands of years.

This book is a primer which gives you simple yet practical ways to develop yourself through soul study and to access thereby the highest powers in the universe. Over the centuries, many people have searched for and wanted this knowledge, but it has never before been brought to the public so openly as within these pages. What you have read will change your life and revolutionize the way you think and act.

We are in the midst of a global upheaval as the 21st century begins. The world as we know it will soon cease to exist. Much is slated to happen. Those who know how to communicate with the universe will be better equipped to adjust to the message and energy of the new millennium.

I bow before heaven for being given the opportunity to prepare the public for this knowledge. It has been my privilege and honour.

Thank you very much.

Thank you.

Testimonials and Comments

From abdominal pains to taking a punch in the belly!

I am very grateful to Master Sha for healing my little girl. At 2 p.m. today, the school called me to come and pick up Natalie, my seven-year-old daughter. She had been complaining of severe abdominal pains for a few hours.

An hour later, her abdomen was so tender that I became really wor- **143** ried. I called Master Sha to see if I could bring Natalie to his office. He told me to relax, asked for her name and age, and then did soul healing for her over the phone. After a few minutes, my little girl jumped up and told me that she was not hurting anymore. She asked me to punch her belly to see for myself. I did!

Ginette Carter
North Vancouver, BC

From a skeptic's point of view, I have gained much...

I am very excited about the progress I have made in the last month. From the point of view of a skeptic, I have gained much understanding and have changed a lot, I hope!

Rudolf Spahman
Summerland, BC

Fibromyalgia and Chronic Fatigue

To Whom It May Concern:

When I met Master Sha in the beginning of March, 1996 for my first treatment, I had been dealing with fibromyalgia for the past 15 years. At the age of 29, I felt like an old and sick person.

144

I have seen many doctors of the western medical profession, as well as different health care professionals in the alternative holistic healing professions, but nobody has been able to help me. Most doctors don't know how to treat fibromyalgia, which only adds to the already existing feeling of hopelessness and depression that goes along with many other symptoms of the disease, such as severe joint and muscle pain, migraine headaches, nausea, insomnia, weakened immune system, short concentration span, loss of memory, and chronic fatigue.

When I came to Master Sha, I was at the end of my rope and had pretty much accepted that I was going to feel like I did then for the rest of my life. On my worst days, I was so tired of everything that all I wanted was to sleep and never wake up again. I have seen Master Sha now for one month and have just completed my second Soul Study weekend. Yeahhhhhhhhhh!

The change in my physical, mental, emotional, spiritual health is simply amazing. I have more energy than in the past 15 years, my muscle and joint pain has improved immensely, I have fewer headaches, and I can sleep through the night. My concentration has improved and most important of all – I'm so very happy and thankful to be alive!!! I'm looking forward to every new day with curiosity and excitement. It truly is a miracle and I feel so blessed.

Nathalie Thomann

Vancouver, BC

Car accident gave insights into the soul world

Recently, I was in a very strange car accident that gave me new insights into the soul world. I hit a lamp standard on an exit ramp coming off the highway. My head broke the windshield and I have some lower back pain from compression trauma. Diana, my passenger, suffered a broken sternum. The lamp standard was knocked off its stand and the bottom of the car and other parts were left strewn in the wake. Diana and I could very easily have died. The investigating officer said that we were lucky to be alive.

The bone specialist who x-rayed Diana's sternum told her that she would be in a lot of pain for the next few months. During Diana's overnight stay in the hospital, we sent her long-distance soul healing. The next day, her bone specialist was amazed at her relatively pain-free state and with her mobility. What impressed me was that Diana was able to pinpoint the exact time we sent the healing, because she could feel her pain lifting and the constriction loosening in her sternum.

Later, in Soul Study class, we studied what had happened with the car accident and I learned that we were saved by higher powers. I feel very fortunate that this was the case for I know that we most certainly would not be here today, if not for their intervention.

Jim Chow

North Vancouver, BC

Today I experienced tears of joy...

Today I experienced tears of joy several times for many reasons. Now I know the names of two of my spiritual guides. I made progress translating the soul language. I heard my soul talking to me about my future plans. I communicated with my mother's soul in South America. The most significant blessing of the weekend was being under the loving and compassionate presence of Sister Dulce, a Brazilian Saint. Wow! What is next?

Ben da Silva

North Vancouver, BC

Reduced hospital stay for pancreatitis...

Two weeks ago, at midnight on Wednesday, I was admitted to hospital for pancreatitis, given three shots of morphine to handle the pain, and put on intravenous fluid. My amylase test measured over 4900. (An amylase count of 200 to 300 is normal.)

The next morning at 9 o'clock, after receiving my first long-distance healing by telephone from Master Sha, I felt more relaxed. I also felt a very warm, tingling sensation in my upper abdomen. When the doctor saw me half an hour later, he was surprised that my amylase count had dropped down to 1100, as it normally only decreases at a rate of 500-700 counts per day. I was put on a clear liquid diet, which normally doesn't happen until the pancreas stabilizes after three days of morphine and IV fluids. This is an amazing improvement.

Master Sha gave me a second long-distance healing by telephone just before noontime that same day. Right away, I felt perkier! I felt more energetic and much better. I was able to leave only two and a half days after admittance to the hospital, instead of the four-day stay that is typical for pancreatitis. I was totally amazed and even the doctor said, "You heal fast, don't you?"

Although I received only two long-distance healings from Master Sha by telephone, I continued to feel the effects for the next few weeks. The abdominal swelling that accompanies pancreatitis usually takes a few weeks to disappear, but this time it was gone in a few days! I credit my speedy recovery entirely to the long-distance healing I received from Master Sha.

Holly Meadows
Vancouver, BC

Cancer lesions greatly reduced...

I was diagnosed with cancer in 1989, and told it had spread to the liver and other organs. One doctor said that I had about three and a half months to live. I changed my life around. I changed my eating habits and became a vegetarian. I didn't get any worse, but I didn't get any better.

In 1993, I met Master Sha at the Cancer Clinic in Vancouver where I was undergoing chemotherapy and radiation. He showed me a simple visualization to use, which was to picture the cancer leaving my body and being dumped into a garbage container about 10 feet away. As one can filled up, I was to replace it with a new container.

Since that day, I have been doing this visualization every morning after I meditate. I also use the *One Hand Near, One Hand Far* hand position for energy balancing. I meditate about beautiful, restful things such as calm ocean scenes, sunsets, flowers. I can actually smell them! After my meditation, when I am perfectly relaxed, I start the visualization of tossing out the cancer cells from my body. This takes about 20 minutes, and then I am ready for my day.

Now, the lesions on my liver are greatly reduced and the ones in my pancreas have remained the same size since 1993. The last time I went to see my oncologist in December of 1995, he asked me what I was doing so I explained Master Sha's method to him. He looked surprised, but did not say anything. I will be seeing him again in three months time and I anticipate he'll be surprised again at the improvement in my condition.

I believe in mind over matter. I believe that there is nothing that the human mind cannot achieve, if it truly believes in what can be achieved.

Lynn Collins
Vancouver, BC

150

I was able to communicate with my daughter's soul

I have believed all my life that I had a special purpose and I have found it in the Soul Study class.

After two weeks of training, I am very excited to have developed my soul language to the point where I have begun to bring healing to my family and to the kindergarten children with whom I work.

Something that has given me great happiness and joy this weekend was being able to communicate with my daughter's soul. My heart rejoices at this gift from the soul world.

Mireille Houle
North Vancouver, BC

Five people treated over the phone...

On Monday, the phone started ringing and I had five different people complaining about different things. I gave them all soul healing over the phone. Each said that he or she received much help almost instantly.

One lady, who was in grief from just losing her sister, felt better after the healing. Another lady felt much better emotionally after I treated her. I was also able to help one man get relief from his cough, and to relieve the pain my husband felt in his back, legs and feet. Another lady, with atypical cervical cells, possibly pre-cancerous, felt warmth and tingling in the area when I treated her. Yesterday, a man who had a pain in his knees for 30 years was instantly healed and is still OK.

151

I'm so excited and grateful about people getting better. I'm delighted to be a participant in the Soul Study group and feel that much good will come from this for everyone involved.

Joyce Stevenson
Vancouver, BC

Direct Communication from the soul world

(as communicated through Sharon Soubolsky)

What is *Te*? How can I increase my *Te*?

Te, *Te*, *Te*, What am I? *Te*, *Te*, I am *Te* and I am the universal message and the universal connection to the whole world and I am what it takes to bring all the union and all the togetherness of all the people coming together. *Te* is the strongest energy vibration that you can ever receive in the whole world and I go through and I hold hands with everybody's soul and I smile upon you and I give you *Te* and *Te* is love, compassion, fighting your selfishness, compassion, compassion, sincere and honesty. It is the place to be and I have so much fun as I journey through life practising and strengthening my *Te* and how I increase my *Te* is I just go and I go and I wake up and I say thank you, thank you, thank you for everything that I have given, received and I thank my Master Sha and all the saints above for bringing me awake in this morning and then I go and I play and I play and I play and I go out and I touch the souls of other people and I see the smiles that come on their faces. I show them how to be sincere and honest and how to fight their selfishness and it just makes me become a stronger and stronger and stronger and better person and I can go and go and have the best time of my life and I've never been so happy in all my life as I am *Te* and I go and I go and I go and I have so much fun because all is love, compassion, humility, honesty, sincerity and as I go I have a commitment to everyday. Every day I want to do better and better and better and as I do better, I become stronger and I become better and I go and serve the people in the world. I want to serve the people. And this is how I do it. *Te* is my heart and *Te* is the connector that gives me and lets me go throughout the whole world so my name is *Te*. Thank you, thank you, thank you.

Sharon Soubolsky

Vancouver, BC

Appendices

Master Guo's Background

Master Zhi Chen Guo first started learning the martial arts and *Qi Gong* at the age of ten. He is now one of China's most famous *Qi Gong* masters. After more than thirty years of practice, he created *Dong Yi Gong*, the Zhi Neng medicine style of *Qi Gong*. He is also a doctor of traditional Chinese medicine, and he has studied and practiced western medicine.

157

In 1986, Master Guo established a *Qi Gong* school in Shijiazhuang City, Tian Jing, China, as a centre for the study of Zhi Neng medicine, *Dong Yi Gong*, and soul study. Combining the essential components of western medicine, traditional Chinese medicine, *Qi Gong*, and his own extraordinary functioning of the senses, he created a revolutionary new health science. In 1992, in front of an audience of thousands, Master Guo formally introduced the principles, theories and techniques of Zhi Neng medicine to the public. These included concepts and practices never before introduced, to develop and balance energy in the body, mind and soul.

Master Guo developed the fast, effective and simple techniques presented in this book and has successfully taught soul study to thousands of people. This study includes soul development, soul communication and soul healing. Highly developed people have applied their soul knowledge to obtain excellent results in many fields such as the health-related professions, mathematics, physics, agriculture, and business enterprises.

Recently, Master Guo has been studying the *zhong gong,* the life centre and basis of a person's life. He has determined that the *zhong gong* is

located behind the portal vein, that it has no shape and is not a solid organ. It glows with a golden, yellow light and radiates many beautiful colours. Your Third Eye needs to be developed to see the *zhong gong.* You are in good health and will have long life if the area is glowing with clear, golden light. When the area is dark and has a blurry image, your health is troubled and your life will be affected.

Finding the *zhong gong* is the latest of Master Guo's contributions to the world. Zhi Neng medicine has spread rapidly throughout China, South Korea, Hong Kong, the Philippines, Singapore and Canada because of the power of his revolutionary insights and theories.

Master Sha's Background

Master Zhi Gang Sha was trained as a doctor in western medicine and in traditional Chinese medicine. He received his MD in western medicine from Xian Medical College, Xian City, Shaanxi Province in 1983 and his Masters' degree in Hospital Administration from the University of the Philippines, in Manila, in 1988. He is also master of many other disciplines, including the *I Ching*, *Qi Gong*, and *Tai Chi Chuan*, having studied under Masters since the age of six.

A highly skilled acupuncturist, Master Sha taught acupuncture to Western doctors in Beijing for the World Health Organization in 1985 and 1986.

In 1979, he developed *Sha's Acupuncture Therapy,* a simplified and streamlined technique that involves energy healing and produces significantly better results than traditional practices. Master Sha has used his revolutionary technique with dramatic results to relieve chronic conditions, pain and debility in thousands of people in China, Hong Kong, the Philippines, the United States and Canada.

As the first disciple and adopted son of Master Zhi Chen Guo, the founder of Zhi Neng medicine, Master Sha has lectured, demonstrated and given seminars on the far-reaching benefits of Zhi Neng medicine to over 100,000 people. Since 1989, he has devoted his life to spreading Zhi Neng medicine to the world. Master Sha established the *International Institute of Zhi Neng Medicine* in Toronto in 1994, and in Vancouver, Canada in 1995.

160

The training Master Sha uses in his Soul Study program was developed by Master Guo. In the Western world, Master Sha is the only master authorized to teach these unique techniques.

The International Institute of Zhi Neng Medicine

The *International Institute of Zhi Neng Medicine* was established in Toronto in 1994 and in Vancouver in 1995 by Master Zhi Gang Sha.

The *International Institute of Zhi Neng Medicine* is a healing centre dedicated to spreading the knowledge, principles and techniques of Zhi Neng   **161**
medicine to the public. Healing of the body, mind and soul is accom-
plished with a combination of *Sha's Acupuncture Therapy*, energy balancing, and soul communication.

The Institute offers practitioner courses and qualifies healers in Zhi
Neng medicine and *Sha's Acupuncture Therapy* from a clinical perspec-
tive. *Dong Yi Gong* classes are offered for energy development and balancing. One-week intensive healing programs are offered as a solution
to chronic pain. Weight loss clinics using Zhi Neng medicine principles
and acupuncture are ongoing. Soul Study, the program upon which this
book is based, was designed by Master Sha to help people to develop
their souls and communication skills with the universe. As well, *feng shui*
classes will soon be added.

A wide range of illnesses are treated in the medical clinic operated by the Institute, including arthritis, asthma, back pain, cancer, cirrhosis of the liver, colds, deafness, diabetes, digestive problems, fibromyalgia, headaches, impotence, incontinence, insomnia, joint pain, menstrual disorders, muscle tension, paralysis following stroke, premature ejaculation, sports injuries, and more. The Zhi Neng medicine family continues to grow as many patients experience true relief from pain for the first time after many years of suffering.

In addition to offering courses and classes in Zhi Neng medicine, energy and soul development, the Institute also has a wide variety of video cassette tapes available for home study. Topics include energy development, *Dong Yi Gong*, weight loss, digestive problems, sinus problems, back pain, headaches and more. Other publications and print materials are also available.

Members of the Institute are often invited to give demonstrations and seminars for hospitals, health organizations, complementary healing centres and other interested parties, locally and internationally. Seminars and demonstrations of Zhi Neng medicine are also held on a regular basis at the Institute and are open to the public.

Please direct any queries on seminar arrangements to the International Institute of Zhi Neng Medicine. We welcome all opportunities to spread the knowledge of this 21ˢᵗ Century Medicine.

Thank you.

163

The International Institute of Zhi Neng™ Medicine
Box #60583
Granville Park PO
Vancouver, BC Canada
V6H 4B9

In North America, call toll-free: 1-888-339-6815

Zhi Neng Press

Revolutionary Healing
Books and Videos by Zhi Gang Sha

Books

Soul Study
A Guide to Accessing Your Highest Powers
ISBN 0-9680595-1-1

Zhi Neng Medicine
Revolutionary Self Healing Methods from China
ISBN 0-9680595-0-3

Sha's Golden Healing Ball
The Perfect Gift
ISBN 0-9680595-3-8

Videos

Beyond Chi I
Energy Boosting & Balancing
Zhi Neng™ Medicine Dong Yi Gong Exercise
with Master Zhi Gang Sha
ISBN 0-9680595-4-6

Order through your local bookstore or from Zhi Neng™ Press.
Call Toll-Free 1-888-339-6815.

ZHI NENG PRESS
VANCOUVER, BC